LET THE LORD BUILD THE HOUSE

8 Steps to Successful Pastoral Planning

LET THE LORD BUILD THE HOUSE

8 STEPS TO *successful* PASTORAL PLANNING

DANIEL S. MULHALL

TWENTY THIRD *23rd*
PUBLICATIONS
NEW LONDON, CT 06320
WWW.23RDPUBLICATIONS.COM

TWENTY-THIRD PUBLICATIONS
A Division of Bayard
One Montauk Avenue, Suite 200
New London, CT 06320
(860) 437-3012 or (800) 321-0411
www.23rdpublications.com

Cover image ©iStockphoto.com/Jovana Cetkovic

Library of Congress Cataloging-in-Publication Data
Mulhall, Daniel S.
  8 steps to successful pastoral planning : let the Lord build the house / Daniel Mulhall.
    p. cm.
  ISBN 978-1-58595-832-0
1. Pastoral theology. 2. Planning. I. Title. II. Title: Eight steps to successful pastoral planning.
  BV4211.3.M85 2012
  254—dc23
                    2011052442

ISBN 978-1-58595-832-0
Printed in the U.S.A.

CONTENTS

If the Lord does not build a house

If you were about to build a house, would you start without a plan? Of course not. Every house needs an effective design, where all the elements fit together, and a pattern to follow that will bring the design to life. Most houses start with a blueprint. A blueprint offers a clear picture of what you hope to build, seen from every conceivable angle, so that you can see how the building will look when the work is completed. The blueprint makes clear the steps needed to complete the project, the order in which these steps are to be taken, and all of the resources you will need to finish the larger job.

STEPS TO SUCCESSFUL PLANNING

There are various books available that tell you how to plan and that walk you through a step-by-step planning process. This book is different: it seeks to teach you how to think about effective planning.

Over many years of work at the parish, diocesan, and national levels, I have been involved in many different kinds of projects. Most

I

of the time it seemed that these projects took on a life of their own, able to continue without much effort being invested in the planning process, or in spite of any planning that may have occurred. At other times, significant amounts of time were wasted as people fought over the wording of a vision or mission statement, only to see that same statement totally disregarded when it came time to set goals and objectives. Far too often, when goals and objectives were set, nothing was done to evaluate how fully the goals and objectives were ever accomplished, or whether accomplishing the goals and objectives actually achieved the desired results.

Once you've learned to think about the planning process in the way I'll explain, you will be ready to take on a step-by-step approach to planning that will have lasting results. I'll lead you through the basics of a step-by-step approach at the conclusion of the book and also offer you suggestions for planning guides that I think you might find of value.

I have organized this book around the steps one would follow if one were building a house (or a church, or a donut shop). Start now by imagining a set of blueprints. What do you see? Obviously, white lines on a blue background (thus the name, blueprint). But what is the importance of a blueprint?

BACK TO THE BLUEPRINT

1. The image of a blueprint   In his book *The Fifth Discipline: The Art and Practice of the Learning Organization* (originally published in hardcover in 1990 by Currency Doubleday, a division of Bantam Doubleday Dell Publishing Group, Inc. Revised 2006), MIT professor Peter Senge names five disciplines that are inherent in a successful learning organization and necessary for systemic thinking. One of those five disciplines is the ability to develop mental models.

For me, this is the discipline most essential to effective planning and the discipline that most planners seem least capable of grasping. The approach to planning offered here is based upon using mental models; you will be asked to form mental models throughout these pages. So, let's get started.

2. The eight steps to successful planning   Here are the eight steps to effective planning that I will address in this book:

1. Know what you want to accomplish (Vision)
2. Know the context where this vision will be realized (Setting)
3. Put your plans in writing (Blueprint)
4. Get the necessary "permits" (Approvals)
5. Start at the beginning and work your way to the top (Organization and Implementation)
6. Remember the "money thing" (Finances)
7. Use the right tools for the job (Programs)
8. How are you doing? (Evaluation)

There's nothing arcane about any of these steps, and they don't require specialized knowledge. Most of what I will present is based upon common sense and practical experience. My father has been in the remodeling and repair business for most of his adult life, and while I did learn to read blueprints growing up, I in no way am a skilled building craftsman—I can hear my brothers, who are skilled builders, laughing at that thought. But I am a skilled craftsman when it comes to planning. This book shares with you what I've learned.

3. Pastoral planning or catechetical planning?   Planning is planning. Groups often get mired down when they think that different tasks require different kinds of planning. Nothing could be further from the truth. The steps that I lay out in this book apply just as effectively to any project, whether it's developing a pastoral or a catechetical plan: the planning process should be relatively the same. Because most of my experience has been in catechesis, most of my stories and references will come out of catechesis. However, I will attempt to make the pastoral planning application apparent in every case. I will also have application questions for you to discuss at the end of each major section of the book. This will provide you with the opportunity to practice the approaches for both pastoral and catechetical planning. What I can't do is address every possible scenario or situation. Ultimately, it will be up to you, the reader, to make the connections.

■　　　■　　　■

When I begin a workshop, I usually begin with song. When doing a planning workshop, I frequently sing the Dan Schutte/St. Louis Jesuit song "If the Lord Does Not Build a House." Although not sung frequently today, the song captures for me what has to be at the heart of all pastoral planning: that the work we do, we do under God's direction, trusting that through God's involvement, our work will achieve lasting significance. The song puts to music the words of Psalm 127:1.

> If the Lord does not build a house,
> Then in vain do the builders labor,
> And in vain do the watchmen stand their guard.
> If the Lord is not their help,
> If the Lord is not their help.
> ◆ Dan Schutte, copyright 1979

So, as we begin this process together, let us keep in mind that it is the Lord who guides our efforts and it is the Lord who will see to our success—as long as we give it our best efforts and do the work we need to do in order to plan effectively.

Daniel S. Mulhall

June 6, 2011

Getting started
Systemic planning

The purpose of this book is to help you to apply systemic thinking to the systems that exist within your parish. This isn't necessarily the approach we take when we talk about planning. For example, during the course of any given day, I'm likely to say "Here's my plan" a dozen or more times. What do I mean by this? Each time I say it I am telling someone that there are things that I want to do and that I have some ideas about how to accomplish them. Or my wife might ask, "Do you have any plans for dinner?" Usually I don't, so we have to talk about it until something comes to mind.

I would suggest that this is what most people mean when they talk about planning: (1) they have an idea in mind as to what they want to accomplish, and (2) they also have some idea as to how they might reach the desired outcome.

Now, such an approach to planning is certainly acceptable when it comes to determining what to have for dinner, whether to choose paper or plastic at the grocery store, or even what you TiVo tonight. But such an approach is totally unacceptable once the project becomes even slightly more complex or important. A more substantial form of planning is necessary in these cases, a form that I call "systemic planning."

Systemic planning occurs when you take a problem (or an opportunity or a project), examine the situation as fully as possible to understand the various components involved—the potential return on your investment of time and money, and the risks you might run—and then develop the detailed steps needed to achieve the desired outcome. Deciding what to have for dinner doesn't fit into this definition; determining what you need to eat in order to lose twenty-five pounds does.

WHAT IS SYSTEMIC PLANNING?

The idea of systemic planning grows out of the work of systems thinkers, people such as Peter Senge, a senior lecturer at MIT, in his book *The Fifth Discipline: The Art and Practice of the Learning Organization.* According to Senge, "Systems thinking is a conceptual framework, a body of knowledge and tools that has been developed over the past fifty years, to make the full patterns clearer, and to help us see how to change them effectively" (p. 7). It is the "discipline of seeing wholes"; it is the "framework for seeing interrelationships rather than things, patterns of change rather" than episodic events (p. 68).

We are surrounded by systems, from the largest—the ecosystem, the way that all of nature is intertwined so that if one part is damaged, the entire system is affected in some way—to smaller systems, for example, the connection of pipes in your home or office that carry cold and hot water. As long as the water flows into your house from an outside source and the series of pipes that carry it don't leak, you will have water at your demand simply by twisting a knob or faucet.

Simple systems are easier to fix than are complex systems, but quick fixes frequently don't solve the problems. For example, let's say the water pressure in your house has been dropping over time. The first thing you'll probably try is to replace the old faucet that has become clogged with mineral deposits. But eventually, to really fix the problem, you will need to tear out all of the pipes in your home and run new ones because the minerals have clogged the pipes as well. The only permanent fix is to install a water purification system at the point where the water enters your home, to cleanse the minerals from the water before they block the pipes. However, the cost of installing and maintaining such a system—which has now become much more complex—may be more expensive than putting in new pipes every fifty years or so. The system gets even more complex when you add the threat of poisoning caused by the lead solder in the joint connections or the toxic chemicals that can leach out of plastic pipes.

See just how complex even a simple system can be? How much more complex are systems that have many more variables?

When you begin to think in systems, the way you see the world changes. Instead of seeing individual puzzle pieces, the puzzle as a whole starts to come into view: you begin to see the "big picture," and how seemingly unrelated events are actually interconnected. It's easy in hindsight to see how a decision that might appear insignificant at the time has led to significant problems. The challenge is to see the big picture in advance and to plan for the results you want. That's the idea behind systemic planning: learning to see all the interconnected pieces of a project prior to an activity and to recognize how they interrelate, and then to work to have them build upon each other so that you can make intelligent decisions about how to address important situations and critical problems effectively.

Here's an example of a simple system that frequently causes problems in parishes: the person who answers the phone or the door in the parish office or rectory (the parish website and answering machines also fit into this discussion). This person is often the first contact the parish has with strangers, seekers, or people in need. How much thought is given to the realization that the receptionist or secretary is an essential part of the parish outreach system and a key member of the parish evangelization program? What happens when this person is rude, obnoxious, or simply not very interested—as we all can be on bad days—or simply extremely busy, underpaid, or poorly prepared for the job? Frequently, the answer is that callers or visitors leave with a bad experience of your parish in their minds. Hopefully, that's not the result you desire. Yet, unless you think systemically, you probably wouldn't consider this person's role in the parish's evangelization efforts.

I've given many workshops over the years on the topic of systemic planning, mostly to people employed as parish catechetical leaders. It is not unusual during these workshops for eyes to light up, for people to grin, and for heads to nod in agreement as these leaders catch on to the concepts I offer and they see the benefits that can be gained from using this approach. As one catechetical leader commented, "I just realized that what I've been doing all of these years isn't planning"—and this from a person widely recognized as one of the best catechetical leaders in that diocese.

Actually, this leader is not alone: most people have little or no concept about what systemic planning is, how they should do it, or why it would be important to do. But that doesn't mean that she wasn't planning, just that she was using a different planning approach, one that I call "episodic planning." In this process, individual events or activities are seen as unrelated, and so the planning focuses on each event as a separate episode.

There is nothing wrong with episodic planning, in and of itself. In fact, you will see many of the words associated with episodic planning—vision and mission and goals and objectives—used in this book. But episodic planning too easily leads to restricted thinking. People become so focused on accomplishing individual goals that they lose sight of what these goals are trying to accomplish. With episodic planning, individual goals take on a life of their own and can replace the larger intended outcome the goals were originally developed to accomplish.

EXAMPLE 1 ▶ EPISODIC PLANNING

St. Clement's Parish decided that it wanted to build a new gym so that it could sponsor a youth volleyball league and keep their young people busy during the summer. The parish designed the gym, raised the money, built the gym, and hosted the league. Three years later the parish had to give up the league because they no longer had enough children in the proper age range to field a team. So now the gym sits unused, except for large parish functions when the extra space is needed.

What was the problem with St. Clement's planning process? Their goal was to build the gym, and the gym got built. Mission accomplished, right? But nowhere in the process did the parish planners look at the reasons for building the facility. No one stopped to ask how building the gym might fit into the parish's mission or how the volleyball league would be a part of the parish's youth program. They, like many others engaged in parish planning, saw a need and addressed the need. Case closed.

The ramifications of such planning should be obvious. If attention had been paid to the parish's demographics, they would have learned that the number of children in that age range was shrinking. This didn't require an expensive study; all anyone needed to do was to check the number of infant baptisms the parish reported to the diocese each year. If you see the numbers dropping for five years running, you know that you won't have many children down the road in that age category. (The rule of thumb is that people moving into and people moving out of a community balances out across age categories—unless, of course, there is some other significant event within the community that would cause large numbers of people to move in or out, such as a major industry opening or closing, or when a tornado destroys half the town.)

To find a real example of this scenario, you need look no farther than the crisis that hit Catholic elementary schools in the 1970s. Without question, the schools were hit hard by the numbers of women and men religious who left teaching at that time and the corresponding cost increases (due to hiring lay teachers) that led to higher tuition rates, driving away many people who had previously never paid much, if any, tuition. Some of these events could not have been anticipated and so could not have been addressed through planning. However, looking back at the historical data from that period, you find a very illuminating bit of information: between 1965 and 1978 the number of births across the United States hit almost historic lows. This was the period now known as the "baby bust." Both public and Catholic schools were hit hard by the lack of elementary-age children, just as high schools were a few years later. It wasn't just that children were being withdrawn from Catholic schools; there also weren't as many potential students available as there had been a few years before. So, many schools that were planned and built to accommodate the record numbers of students of the late 1950s and early 1960s stood almost empty by the 1970s. This lack of students turned a very difficult situation into a near catastrophe for many parishes.

The biggest difference between episodic planning and systemic planning is where the focus of the planning is put. Episodic planning is concerned with events or episodes, while systemic planning is concerned with the parish as a system, as a whole collection of activities and events, people and their varied lives, and all the other aspects of the Church's liturgical and spiritual life. The systemic planner recognizes that many, if not all, events that happen within the parish are connected in some way. The episodic planner is only concerned with the project at hand.

In *The Fifth Discipline*, Peter Senge calls systems thinking the "conceptual cornerstone" that helps us to restructure how we think. It helps us to move from being "helpless reactors" to becoming actors capable of "creating the future" (p. 69). According to Senge, in order to do this, we must (1) move from a linear cause and effect way of seeing the world to one where we can see the interrelationships between situations and events. Then we must (2) learn "to see a process of change rather than snapshots" or episodes (p. 73). Such systemic thinking will help us to do systemic planning.

Seeing the big picture

What do I mean by the big picture? Let's return to the example above of St. Clement's Parish. Here are the big-picture questions I'd ask the parish, listed in the order in which I'd ask them.

1. Why does St. Clement's exist as a parish?
2. What makes people want to belong to St. Clement's?
3. What is it that you want St. Clement's to become as a parish?
4. What results would you expect to see in each age group in the parish in order to show that your efforts are being successfully implemented?
5. What needs to happen to get those results (i.e., change of attitude, conversion, commitment, etc.)?
6. What are things that you can do to achieve those results?
7. Where is the best place to start to achieve these results?

In episodic planning the starting point is often "What do we want to do?" or "What do we need to do?" "What do we have to do?" or even, "What are we currently doing?" Those questions don't even make the initial list in a systemic planning perspective. They would eventually be asked as part of the planning process, but that's not where I'd start the conversation, and they certainly wouldn't be the deciding factor.

Again, the key questions of systemic planning have to do with desired outcomes: What do you want to accomplish? How will accomplishing that help you to accomplish your larger goals? How will accomplishing your larger goals lead to your achieving your big-picture intended outcome?

Use the following questions to help you work your way through a system in your parish. I'll offer the situation; your task is to identify the different parts of the system involved. Don't try to fix the problem yet—simply trace the system and see where it leads.

Situation: People complain about traffic problems in the parking lot before and after Sunday Mass.

▶ *What can you observe?*

> Timing of problems
> Traffic patterns
> Speed of traffic
> Traffic on road that leads to parking lot
> Number of cars at each Mass
> Number of spaces for cars
> Parking pattern
> Time between Masses
> How quickly people leave lot at the end of Mass
> Times when people stay longer than at other times
> How early people arrive at the beginning of Mass
> Other activities occurring during Mass times
> Number of cars associated with these extra activities
> How pedestrians interfere with traffic flow

▶ *Questions to ask:*

- How would reconfiguring the parking lot ease the traffic flow?
- What can be done to get people to arrive at Mass earlier and leave more slowly at the end?
- Is there a need for more parking?
- Is there a need for someone to direct traffic?
- Would a different pick-up and drop-off space help solve the problem?
- Would more time between Masses help? Is this possible?

▶ *What other questions do you feel need to be asked?*

As you can see, there are many questions to answer before you can even begin to plan to solve the problem. The key is to remember that you start by trying to understand the bigger picture before deciding on a solution. Perhaps part of the solution is to offer coffee and donuts between Masses to get people to hang around longer and thus stagger the traffic flow, or perhaps a satellite parking lot with free shuttle service might be needed. But real solutions are not possible until you understand how the "traffic system" at your parish works.

One of my favorite quotations is attributed to Albert Einstein: "Insanity: doing the same thing over and over again and expecting different results." By this standard, most of us would be certifiable, for we continue to do the same things hoping that next time our results will be different. They won't be; they can't be. The only way that we will get the results we desire in our parishes and in our catechetical programs is if we change the way we think about our work, change the way we go about doing our work, and ultimately, change the way we plan.

Remember one thing: whatever solution you find for this problem may also be the cause of other problems or address other problems elsewhere in the parish. So consider the further ramifications of the actions before implementing any solutions. This will be addressed more fully in a later chapter.

See Appendix I for a hypothetical case study of how systemic planning asks different and more effective questions than episodic planning.

■ Discussion questions

- ▶ What's the biggest event that you've ever planned? A wedding? A parish retreat or outing? A ten-day family vacation? Your career?
- ▶ How detailed was your plan? Was it written or drawn? Did you have a mental image of what you hoped to accomplish?
- ▶ How effective was your plan? How did you determine its success?
- ▶ Where did your planning break down?
- ▶ Where did it succeed?
- ▶ Are you an episodic planner or a systemic planner? How can you tell?

Know what you want to accomplish (*Vision*)

"We may be very busy, we may be very efficient, but we will also be truly effective only when we begin with the end in mind."

◆ Stephen R. Covey, *Seven Habits of Highly Effective People*

Although each and every step in the planning process is very important, none is more important than this first step. This is where you establish your vision and where you identify what you want to accomplish. The clarity of your vision here will determine the final outcome of your labor.

VISION OR MISSION STATEMENTS

In most planning processes you start by developing a mission statement or a vision statement. I find that while most parishes have mission and/or vision statements, few actually are guided by these statements. When I ask at workshops if their parishes have mission statements, most participants say, "yes." When I ask if they base their planning on the statement, most look at me as if I'm from outer space, as if they'd never heard of such a crazy idea. But unless your planning is guided by the vision of what you want to accomplish and how you plan to accomplish it, your planning is doomed from the start—okay, maybe not doomed, but certainly seriously hampered by lack of focus.

What exactly is a mission or vision statement meant to accomplish? What is the proper relationship between mission and vision, and goals and objectives? How is it that we can accomplish objectives but yet never accomplish our goals, or that we can accomplish our goals but never achieve our intended outcome?

If you search the internet for the words "mission statement" and "vision statement," you will come up with many different and often confusing answers. One person's definition of a mission statement could easily be confused with another's definition of a vision statement. Some people encourage you to start by writing a vision statement and move from there to describe your mission, while others recommend that you do exactly the opposite. Such is the English language. As there is no clear arbiter on this matter, I offer my own understanding of these two concepts.

For me, mission statements come first. They present clearly and succinctly a group's purpose for existing. They should include meaningful and measurable criteria and concepts about the group, such as its moral and ethical position, its public image, whom it seeks to serve, and how it seeks to serve. Said in another way, mission statements describe who a group is and why it exists. Mission statements are important: they should guide every decision a group makes.

Vision implies the ability to see, to look ahead and know where you are going, to understand what you want to accomplish. The clearer your vision is, and the more concretely you can express it, the easier it will be for you to determine what steps you need to take to accomplish it. In general, most vision statements seem to fall short in this category. They do not describe what the group actually hopes to accomplish—and that's the rub.

Vision and mission not only tell us where we are going, they also define for us what we do and how we do it.

Simply put, a mission statement establishes who you are (e.g., People of God), what you are (e.g., formed into a community of faith), and why you are (e.g., in order to bring the Good News to others), while a vision statement explains what you hope to accomplish (e.g., build a community of believers committed to living the Christian life) and how you hope to accomplish it (e.g., through prayer, worship, fellowship, and Christian service). These statements are often combined into one and are usually written, although they don't have to be. But they must be known by all, owned by all, and followed by all. By that I mean every event and activity in the parish should be aimed, in some way, at accomplishing the mission and goal. What's important is that the parish has an idea of where it is going and how it is going to get there.

Unfortunately, writing mission or vision statements can become exercises in futility. Processes often break down into arguments over words and phrases. This is another example of episodic thinking. The intent is for the parish to determine who it is, what it is, and why it exists; writing a mission statement is only a strategy used to get there. Yet, producing the statement is often the only outcome; it doesn't affect how the parish lives in any way. I've belonged to parishes that had glowing mission statements but whose actual reason for existing based upon where all the money and effort went—

youth sports—was never even suggested in the statement. Or parishes whose vision statement was (in my words) "All are welcome," but whose attitude and programming said "except for families with young children, divorced and remarried couples, people from other countries, and anyone else who doesn't fit our sense of propriety."

VISION VS. MISSION
CATECHETICAL MINISTRY IN YOUR PARISH

Which vision of church would you select?

(1) "That all parishioners would experience the saving power of our Lord, Jesus Christ, come to know and love him through the life of the community, and choose to follow him as faithful disciples."

(2) "That all parishioners would be given the opportunity to experience the saving power of our Lord, Jesus Christ, come to know and love him through the life of the community, and choose to follow him as faithful disciples. Those who choose to follow his teaching would be welcomed into the parish community."

The first vision aims to bring all people to Christ. Those who live out this mission would not be satisfied if even one person living within the parish failed to fall in love with Christ and his Church. Those operating out of the second vision would be satisfied as long as adequate opportunities were provided. If people didn't come to faith, well, that's not our problem. Understand, I'm not saying that one vision is better than another, but simply that we need to be clear about what our vision is.

Lacking a clear vision is a major problem in most parishes and catechetical programs. Even more troublesome, though, is having a stated vision, but then operating out of an unstated one.

For example, a parish's vision statement says that they "wish to be a place where all are welcome." What would the parish look like if that vision were put in practice? We could expect it to be open, transparent, willing to listen, no distinctions made because of sexuality or lifestyle. Every effort would be made to overcome racial and ethnic prejudices and to have members from various ethnic cultures to shape parish activities so that all would feel welcome. If the parish isn't welcoming in all ways, it is not living out its vision. Also consider the parish that claims to be a justice community and yet treats its employees poorly. Obviously it is important that our lived vision and our stated vision agree with each other.

Again, our mission is our intended outcome; our vision is the way we choose to get there. In other words, while following the path will move us along on our journey, following the path itself is not the intended outcome of our journey. In *The Wizard of Oz*, Dorothy's mission was to get home to Kansas. In order to get there, she had to reach the Emerald City by following the yellow brick road.

In the same way, our sacramental prep programs or adult faith formation sessions are not ends in themselves, but the means we use to achieve our intended results and accomplish our mission. So, what is the end you have in mind? How will you know when you arrive? Suggested intended outcomes might be: "a lifetime of sacramental practice" or "recognizing the importance of the need for lifelong learning toward discipleship."

What is your vision for catechesis or family life or social ministry? What are you trying to accomplish in your parish with the various programs you offer? Take a moment to think about that question before going any further in your reading. Take a clean sheet of paper and write down the two questions and your answers to them.

Some more questions for you to answer on your paper: Does your parish have a mission or vision statement? Where is it? Is it concise enough to memorize? How has it been promoted within the parish? How does this statement affect the work you do? How does what you do help to accomplish this mission or vision?

The parish's catechetical plan is the way that the parish attempts within its catechetical ministry to make the parish vision become a reality. The parish's catechetical ministry should also have a mission and vision statement of its own (as should other ministries within the parish), shaped by the parish's statements, just as the parish's statement should be shaped by the diocese's statement. If the parish doesn't have a vision or mission statement, by all means develop a parish catechetical plan based upon the vision offered in the *General Directory for Catechesis* or the *National Directory for Catechesis*. The same is true for family ministry or ministry with people with special needs, or a stewardship plan. The U.S. bishops have provided guidance for each of these ministries. However, whatever you do, don't determine this plan by yourself. It's the parish's plan, not yours. You must get approval from the proper authorities before you begin this process. I'll write more on this in a later step.

One of the reasons that people seem to have problems with this stage of the planning process is that pastoral or catechetical visions are difficult to fully envision. It's hard to describe what a mature faith would be, although you can identify the results you'd see if parishioners had a mature faith. That's why I use the image of building a house as the way to think about planning, and encourage folks to use the steps in that process to guide the planning. You can also use the image of a journey, as Vatican II suggests when it calls the Church a "Pilgrim People," but I'll stick with the house image for concrete reasons (pun intended).

■ Discussion questions

▶ What is the difference between vision and mission? Why is this difference important?

▶ What role should vision and mission play in a planning process? What roles do they currently play in your current planning?

▶ Assuming you have a vision and/or mission statement, how was this statement created? How well does it reflect the attitude of the entire community?

Know your context
(Setting)

There is an old joke told about real estate: "What is the most important feature for selling a house? The answer: Location, location, location." The same thing applies to successful planning: to be successful a plan must be developed intentionally for the site where the plan is to be implemented. Prepackaged plans that don't reflect local customs, cultures, and values are likely to fail. No matter how well a particular plan might work in one location, there is no reason to believe that it will succeed somewhere else. (That doesn't mean that it can't be adapted for use in a different location, but that is a different topic.)

To think about this concretely, imagine the house of your dreams. Where exactly will the house be located? Will it sit on a hill beside a lake or in a valley in a forest? Would you choose a city neighborhood near a museum or library, or would you choose a rural setting far from modern civilization?

The point here is this: Where you choose to build will affect what you do and how you do it, along with the costs (in time and money) of what you build. You can't plan on much direct sunlight in a forest unless you cut down trees, and sitting on a hill exposes a house to all the elements. So location affects everything in your building process.

The same is true for your planning process: The context of your parish will affect what you can accomplish, the speed at which you can accomplish it, and what the costs will be. So, as you begin to plan you need a good idea of the "lay of the land" in your parish. What do you know about the parishioners? What is the culture of the parish? Is there more than one culture in the parish? More than one language? What is its history? What are the demographics now and what are they projected to be in ten years? Are your parishioners, in general, highly educated or not? Does the parish consider itself white-collar or blue-collar? Are parishioners used to giving orders or taking them? Is the parish actively involved in social ministry or focused more on internal issues? This is only the tip of the iceberg.

Understanding your parish context will allow you to plan more effectively, and by so doing, avoid a lot of later difficulties. What stumbling blocks should you know about so you can plan around them? Imagine the fight you would have if you tried to change first Eucharist from second grade to fifth grade. You get the picture.

DISCOVERING THE LAY OF THE LAND IN YOUR PARISH

Let's begin by examining some of the questions we raised above. What do you know about your parish? Whether you are planning for the parish's long-term future or simply want to improve the way you provide services now, it is important to understand early on in the planning process as much as you possibly can about your parish.

Knowing the parish's history and traditions will give you a better feel for its customs and cultures. Customs and culture are established early and continue to develop across generations. They establish the parish's identity of itself both internally (what it does, how it does it, when and why it does it, and the meaning of everything it does) and externally (how it relates to the world around it).

You may be asking, "Why is this important? How will spending time on this help me to plan more effectively?" Here's why.

THE PARISH AS LIVING ORGANISM

Parish communities are living organisms. Some people serve as the heart of the parish, keeping it alive at all times. Others serve as the brains, the nervous system, the hands, and the feet of the parish. How does this translate into day-to-day operations? These may be the people who you can count on for advice, or money, or to carry out projects and run the festivals, or to participate when called upon. And alongside these folks are the others (just as significant for your purposes): the followers, the ones who sit in back and don't participate, the whiners, the ones who are always too busy.

One way of considering the health of your parish is to find out parishioners' engagement level. In other words, how committed are they to parish life and ministry? How much do they give? How willing are they to make decisions with the parish community in mind?

The Gallup Organization uses a survey instrument called ME25 to measure engagement. It is called this because there are twenty-five questions, to determine just how alive and vital your parish is. It will give you a snapshot of how your parish is today, just like a checkup at the doctor's will tell you how your personal health is doing. And just as your doctor or conditioning coach might prescribe a training routine for getting your body back in good condition, ME25 will provide you with suggestions for increasing the number of actively engaged people in your parish. According to Gallup's research your parish's vitality can be predicted by the number of actively engaged parishioners you have. Here's how parishes stack up:

- The best parishes and churches have thirty-three percent or more of their parishioners actively engaged. These parishes or churches are alive with energy, overcrowded with people (one of the signs of a vitally alive parish is that parishioners are constantly inviting new people to join their church!), and fully engaged with missionary activity both within and outside the church. These parishes have reached a critical mass: there are enough actively engaged parishioners that not a lot of effort has to go into growing the parish; it happens naturally.

- Parishes that are doing well but still have plenty of work to do have more than eighteen percent of their parishioners actively engaged. Obviously, the higher the number of engaged people, the more vital the parish is. A lot of the parish's time is still spent in trying to grow the parish, trying to keep it from slipping, from becoming mediocre, from losing its momentum. But it continually attracts new people—while losing others who are unhappy or disinterested—and has a fairly vibrant and active parish ministry.

- Parishes with fewer than eighteen percent of their members actively engaged face many more challenges. Their congregations are not energetic and alive, they do not attract many new members, and the same people continually do the same ministries. These parishes spend a lot of their time and effort in survival mode, just trying to keep the doors open and the bills paid. What's sad is that, according to Gallup, most Catholic parishes have about twelve to fifteen percent actively engaged parishioners. No wonder so many parishes are experiencing financial difficulties or are at risk of being closed or merged.

Beyond engagement levels, check the parish's mission statement. Some parishes see themselves as welcoming to all, some see themselves as people on a mission, and some see themselves as deeply spiritual. Whether how they see themselves and their lived reality match is unimportant here. What the planner needs to understand is what the parish thinks about itself. It is far better to work with and build upon a community's perceived strength than it is to try to improve its obvious weaknesses.

Finally, just as the body has nerve sensors to let us know when we experience pain, parishes have people who are very aware of changes to parish life and ministry—and who make themselves loudly heard when they feel that important parts of the parish are in danger of harm. Planners need to listen carefully to these people and show them the respect they deserve. If they raise concerns about the harm that might be caused by a particular activity, listen carefully to them. At the same time, however, decisions can't be determined by questions or challenges these sensors raise. Just as you can't gain fitness unless you push your body past its normal stopping point, plans cannot be implemented unless you can move parishioners from their comfort zone.

CHANGE IS DIFFICULT AT ALL TIMES

Parishioners feel a certain ownership and pride in the parish. Perhaps they helped to build its buildings; played or had children play on sport teams that accumulated the trophies in the display case; attended or sent their children to the parish school; received the sacraments or buried a relative from the building. The more actively engaged people are, the stronger their feelings might be, but even people who seem to have only a loose connection to the parish may have many strong bonds to the place. For many, these strong bonds may be the only reason they continue to participate at all in the parish today. For many of these people, even the slightest hint of change might send them into a tailspin.

The more you know about people's concerns and fears, the easier it will be to address their concerns in your plans. Being aware of people's fear of change can be a way of helping you find the words you need to sell the need for broad parish changes effectively.

What planners frequently forget here is that all parishioners have a right to have a voice in how decisions are made and plans implemented. They may never actively offer their concerns or raise their voices to object, but they still have a voice because this is their parish—just as much (if not more so) as it is the bishop's, the pastor's, the parish council's, or the finance committee's. Their observations should be given weight and serious consideration. For plans to be successful they must represent the will of the community.

SYSTEMIC PUSHBACK—OPPOSITION TO IDEAS

Newton's Laws of Physics put it this way: "For every action there is an equal and opposite reaction." Any time you press somewhere within a system, you will get an equal and opposite reaction somewhere else within the system. Perhaps you plan to change Mass times to improve traffic congestion problems in the parking lot. What other problems might this cause? Where might these spring up? The better you know your parish, the more likely it will be that you will anticipate and address these pushbacks.

This is what is known as the Law of Unintended Consequences: Every change you make sets in motion other, unintended changes which lead to results you may not desire. Futurist Joel Barker says that before making any change you should consider what unintended consequences may result from that change—and follow it through five generations. For example: (1) improving the quality of worship will attract more worshipers, (2) more worshipers will bring more cars, (3) more cars means traffic problems, (4) traffic problems means problems with the neighbors or the local government, (5) neighbor/government problems will bring legal expenses and time spent dealing with the problem. And each of these consequences will have its own additional consequences.

By anticipating what these unintended consequences might be you can begin to plan how to deal with them. Perhaps you will find unintended consequences that you can't afford to have happen— for example, if closing a poorly functioning kindergarten program would lead to thirty percent of your young families leaving the parish for another with a kindergarten program, would you make that choice or do something else? Be aware of these consequences and assess them early on in your planning.

Cooperation, collaboration, confrontation

Cooperation, collaboration, and confrontation are the three Cs of relationships. *Cooperators* want to be included in the planning process, but they are happy for it to be on someone else's terms. They will do whatever you want them to do, as long as you spell it out for them. They may have opinions but they generally aren't wedded to them. They are generally do-ers and aren't so interested in reasons or explanations. They are generally pleasant and engaging, very interested and concerned for the parish or group, and value getting along very highly.

Collaborators want to be actively involved in the planning process. They want to help to shape what is done, when it is done, and how it is done. They are very concerned about outcomes and their effects. Collaborators insist on being heard and on having their thoughts and ideas visible in the final plan. They are serious about what is being done and how. Ignore a collaborator at your peril.

Confronter describes both a style of interaction as well as a personality type. People who fall into this category have very strong opinions and they demand to be heard. Their approach is often confrontational, hoping to win arguments by force of lungs and persistence more than by logic and reasoning—the forte of the collaborators. Confronters are often people who are angry with the Church or who are unhappy with a particular act or policy. The book *Growing an Engaged Church*, by Albert L. Winseman (Gallup Press, 2007), refers to these folks as "actively disengaged." They really aren't concerned with what happens with the parish or program. Instead, they want their grievance to be heard and dealt with—although, in many cases, this is no longer possible. Winseman's advice is to listen carefully to these folks but to not let them take up all of your time or overly influence the planning process.

INSIDER OR OUTSIDER

Who are the insiders and outsiders in your parish? Your plan is sure to be received differently based on that criterion. Will it help to bridge the gaps between these two groups? More important, are there systemic reasons why some people feel like outsiders? If so, how can you address this problem and begin to fix it?

SHORT-SIGHTED FIXES CAUSE LONG-TERM PROBLEMS

In *The Fifth Discipline*, Senge describes this issue effectively. He writes that cutting an elephant in half creates a big mess, not two smaller, easier-to-deal-with problems.

As you begin to plan, find out as much as you can about past attempts to fix various problems. Find out what was done, when it was done, how it was done, and what people thought about it. Try to find out what the consequences were from the previous fix: What new problems were caused?

If this is a parish's first attempt at systemic planning, it would not be a surprise to discover that many, if not most, previous fixes addressed outward issues instead of trying to get at the underlying cause. This is like putting a bandage on skin cancer: people now see the bandage and not the blotchy skin, but the cancer continues to eat away underneath. The problems haven't gone away: they've just been forced elsewhere, creating new and usually more difficult problems along the way.

Knowing about these earlier fixes and the additional problems they caused will help you to avoid making the same mistakes, and teach you the value of trying to get to the root causes of any problem you are trying to address. Remember, in this case divide and conquer is not the right advice.

IN IT FOR A LIFETIME

Although our ever-more-mobile world is causing this variable to change, it is important for planners to remember that most parishioners join parishes and stay there for a lifetime. Most parishioners don't "parish shop" once they've found a place they like. They set down roots and make the parish their home. Any plans you make will affect them in some way, just as it would if you announced that you were building a road that had a slight possibility of changing the traffic pattern of their neighborhood. Tread cautiously at all times.

As one friend of mine once said about a new pastor he didn't much care for, "Pastors come and pastors go. I was here before he got here and I'll be here when he leaves. Whatever he does while he is here will probably be undone by the next pastor who comes, so I'll just keep on keeping on." Important advice for planners: take the long-term view. Plan as if what you decide will affect your own home and how you live. Then you will, indeed, tread cautiously at all times.

To review: Here are the questions you need to consider:
- When was your parish founded and by whom?
- What is the history and tradition of the parish?
- Who are the parishioners? How long have they been in the parish?
- Are your parishioners, in general, highly educated or not?
- Does the parish consider itself white-collar or blue-collar?
- Are parishioners used to giving orders or taking them?
- What are the demographics now and what are they projected to be in ten years?
- What is the culture or cultures of the parish? What forms and shapes these cultures?
- What is the parish's identity?
- Is the parish more focused externally (e.g., actively involved

in social ministry) or focused more on internal issues (e.g., sacrament driven)?

- Who are the key groups in the parish?
- Who are the key players; who can smooth your path or stop you in your tracks?

You can never listen too often or too much to the people in your parish. They are the folks you're planning for—make sure the plan fits them!

■ Discussion questions

▶ How does your parish differ from neighboring parishes? How is it similar? What difference should that make in any planning process?

▶ What value is there in knowing the history of the parish before beginning the planning process? How might this knowledge help you to plan more effectively?

▶ What percentage of your parishioners is actively engaged in the life of the parish? Why are they engaged? What would it take to get a greater number of parishioners to become actively engaged? What plan could you put in place to increase this active participation?

▶ Who are the cooperators, collaborators, and confronters in your parish? What can you do to effectively engage them in the planning process? What might each of these groups have to offer of benefit to the planning process? How might each of these groups undermine or hinder the planning process?

▶ What is the value of taking a long-term view? Looking at the proposed planning process: what might the parish be like as a result of it in five years? twenty years? fifty years?

Put your plans in writing
(Blueprint)

Planning is a process that is both dynamic and fluid. A plan doesn't spring fully formed from the head of Zeus (or the committee). Rather, it develops and grows over time. Plans change repeatedly because of several variables: (1) more information is gathered, (2) we become clearer about what we want to accomplish from our planning and the steps we want to take to get there, and (3) we consider and test our ideas against reality.

Plans are dynamic because they are constantly changing. And they are fluid because the people who create them are constantly thinking and expressing their thoughts and then having those thoughts shaped by new experiences and new insights from others.

While plans are both fluid and dynamic, that doesn't mean that planning is without structure. In fact, while freedom is both allowed and encouraged in the visioning part of the planning process, some structure or design is crucial as you proceed. Eventually, plans must be explained with words and images. If you're building a house, you need a set of blueprints to follow. You need an understandable set of guidelines for your plan so that the entire community can see and understand the vision the planning team has seen. If the people can't see and understand the vision, they will not buy into it or support it. In order for them to see and understand your vision, you must be able to show it to them in words and with images.

Creating a written (or drawn) plan serves a number of basic purposes:

- *It helps the planning team develop clarity about what they are proposing.* If they can't explain it to their own satisfaction, how will they ever explain it to the wider community? In her book *Almost Christian*, Kenda Creasy Dean explains that in talking about what we believe we also clarify what we believe. With a written or drawn plan a group can also visualize the outcome of their efforts more easily, which will allow them to focus their efforts more intentionally toward accomplishing that vision.

- *It provides a record of the planning journey.* In the "old days" this record would show a lot of strike-throughs and erasures that showed the thought process of a group. Today, with "correction-checking" software, it is easy to see the changes that were made and when they were made. This is a valuable tool for the planning process. Keeping a record of when an idea first entered the plan, when it was modified or dropped, or when it was approved is invaluable because it not only allows you to track the development of ideas (and who offered them), it also allows you to go back to the beginning and start over whenever that is needed. Such a feature is a great bonus in systemic planning, because you will continually be returning to your starting premise to make sure you haven't varied from your desired outcome.

- *It safeguards the revision process.* The statement, "Dominating people (or groups) tend to dominate," while a tautology, is also true. Dominating people often have strong characters or personalities, which allows them frequently to control situations in which they find themselves. Dominating people are drawn to positions where they can dominate. They don't intend to take over the planning process but they usually do. They don't intend to force their opinions on others, but that happens as well. By having a written vision to consult, one can always correct the dominating person when he or she remembers a decision having gone a different way. You are free to change previous decisions, of course, but keeping the record intact will help you throughout.

What do I need, when do I need it?

Another reason for having your vision down on paper is that you will clearly see how much stuff you need to achieve your dream and when you will need it. For example, if you are building a house, your blueprint shows every stud, every screw, every foot of concrete or electrical wiring, every window, every door, every lock and sash, every tile, every inch of roofing. This allows you to budget much more accurately (more on this in a later chapter). You will need written plans similar in detail to a blueprint if you are going to plan successfully. You need to be able to envision the results of all your labor before you take even one step to move from planning to program.

Blueprints are also valuable because they help you determine what infrastructure work needs to be done before you begin building: Where will the utilities enter the building? When do they need to be brought in? How must the ground be prepared before something can be built on this site? Building can't start until these infrastructure items are addressed. The same is true about planning for starting Bible study in your parish or starting a stewardship campaign. You must first identify the "infrastructure needs" and figure out how they will be handled. This process is made much easier by having a written or drawn plan of action.

Let me offer here one of the best illustrations of this process I've ever read. Scott Raab is the author of a series of essays in *Esquire* Magazine, tracking the progress of the rebuilding process taking place at Ground Zero in New York City. By the Spring of 2011, all of the replacement towers were starting to rise above street level and the 9/11 Memorial was to be finished by the ten-year anniversary. What has been fascinating reading in these articles is the planning process that was necessary to make this project become a reality. Raab offers high praise to Chris Ward, the director of the project, for bringing order out of chaos. According to Raab, Ward "delivered a thirty-four-page report that boiled down to this: Ground Zero's budget and deadlines were so at odds with reality that it would take three months more just to figure out a realistic schedule to finish the rebuilding."

Quoting Ward, Raab writes: "Myopic monumentalism wrecked this project. You can't have a monument in a day. You don't define the project by that at the beginning. You have to build it—and that requires patience. It requires hard work, and it requires deadlines. We know every single day how much steel has to be placed, and how much concrete has to be poured.... And let's just step back here. We've done a lot—we've built 700,000 square feet below grade, we're building an air-conditioning system for 1.8 million square feet of public space. It's a kids' game of pickup sticks—they're tied together. You can't touch one without touching everything else."

One other Ward quote from the Raab article to drive the point home:

"That gray steel over there is the floor of the foundation. We're gonna bring it all the way over to the top here. So while there's still work being done down here, the PATH [commuter train] station ceiling will be there—more importantly, the floor of the memorial'll be there, so we can plant the trees and finish the fountains. We're building from the top down."

Unfortunately, that's not how most planning processes in our parishes work. As suggested earlier, usually someone decides what they want to do without reflecting on how that decision affects the whole, and then develops a process in order to do what they want to do—episodic planning at its finest. And when it fails, no one seems to understand what caused the failure. Some good was achieved, of course: the workshop or class was held, kids received the sacraments, and the project was accomplished, and was even frequently well done. But when the accomplished project doesn't lay the foundation for what you are ultimately trying to develop, it fails.

Your blueprint will help you keep your ultimate goal in mind, and will help you organize the steps you need to achieve it.

■ Discussion questions

- ▶ Can you visualize what you want to accomplish, the "big picture"? What does your vision look like?

- ▶ Can you draw it out on paper or explain what you want to accomplish in writing in a few sentences in such a way that others can see what you see and feel about it what you feel?

- ▶ Does the vision fit with the lay of the land? Will you receive so much opposition from parishioners that accomplishing your plan would be made more difficult?

- ▶ What general steps will you need to take to accomplish your vision and when will you need to take them?

- ▶ How much will it cost in money, time, planning, social and political capital, to accomplish your vision?

Get the necessary permits
(Approvals)

In a building process, permits serve a vital purpose: they allow those in authority to make sure that the project's work is being done according to code—the way it should be done in order to work effectively. That they may also be mere bureaucratic headaches doesn't take away from their reasons for existing. So you get permits before you begin the job, and then those permits get signed off on as parts of the project are finished correctly.

The same thing needs to happen in your planning process. You have to determine which "permits" you need and who needs to approve them. While the pastor or pastoral leader will always be the ultimate signer, every parish will have its own structure for giving approval. You simply need to find out which groups need to be consulted and how frequently they want updates. You will be well served if you develop a strategy for how you plan to get your plans approved.

WHY PERMITS ARE NEEDED

While building permits and the like are intended to protect public safety and other important public values, they also serve another purpose: they help make us aware that even though we may be building this object on private property, anything we do could have an impact on innocent victims. For example, you want to be sure that the deck you're planning on building, or the fence you want to erect, doesn't cross your neighbor's property lines. Land records need to be checked, etc. Requiring permits is the government's way of protecting the broader public. You may not like them, but if you want to get the permissions you need to build what you want to build, you get the necessary permits.

So, what do building permits have to do with your plan to increase giving in your parish, or developing an effective adult formation program, or improving parent involvement in their children's religious education? Actually, quite a lot. First, just as I'm not free to build whatever I want on my property, I'm not free to plan whatever I want in my parish or job. You may be the person charged with developing a plan, but you have to understand that you can't do whatever you want to do. What you do will affect the parish community and so the community has a say in what you do. A good way of thinking about this is that you are not creating *your* plan, you are creating the *parish's* plan. Adopting this perspective will make it much easier for you to consult widely, get input broadly, and accept proposed changes more easily.

Second, just as there are building codes to protect community safety and property rights, the Catholic Church has its own set of codes. The best known of these codes is the Code of Canon Law, which could have some bearing on everything you attempt to do, especially if it has to do with matters concerning physical church property and the rights of clergy. You will want to get advice from a Canon lawyer if your planning process affects these areas.

CODES AND MORE CODES...

The universal Church also provides other documents that serve the same purpose as codes but may not usually be thought of in this way. For example, if you are making plans to affect the way you do evangelization in the parish, you will want to read and study the document *Evangelii Nuntiandi* and the U.S. Conference of Catholic Bishops' (USCCB) evangelization pastoral plan, *Go and Make Disciples*, to see what they call for you to do and how to do it. If you are considering efforts in liturgy, be sure to study carefully the Vatican II document, *Constitution on the Sacred Liturgy*, (*Sacrosanctum Concilium*), as well as the recently published *General Introduction to the Roman Missal, Third Edition*, along with other USCCB documents on the liturgy. If you will be planning in the area of catechetics, you will need to study the Vatican's *General Directory for Catechesis* (1997) and the USCCB's 2005 *National Directory for Catechesis*. There are too many documents and planning aspects to cover them all here. The best advice I can offer is for you to check with your local diocesan office responsible for the areas your plans involve, and ask them for recommendations on the documents you need to read.

Be aware that, unlike civil building codes, most of the Church's codes exist in the area of guidelines: they provide guidance on what should be accomplished and how, but they generally aren't binding, meaning they can't make you do things in certain ways. They can only offer guidance; how you do it is up to you. That said, various dioceses have their own requirements related to every aspect of church life, and some dioceses are far stricter than others. Again, the best advice when beginning your planning process is to check with your local diocesan office to see what diocesan policies relate to what you intend to do. You will usually find these people to be well-trained professionals in their field who are willing to help you in any ways that they can. They generally have no interest or responsibility for approving your plans, but they will certainly be interested in helping your plan be as successful as possible.

Once you know the approval process your diocese requires, it's time to identify the other people in your community who need to be part of the "permit" process.

WHO DOES THE APPROVING?

In every planning process there are at least two layers of approval needed: the official and unofficial. People and groups in the official layer would include anyone in an official level of authority, certainly the pastor. (You will want to speak to him and get his initial approval before you do anything else.) Depending on what is being planned, the parish council will usually be involved. If the plan affects budgets, fundraising, and spending, then the parish financial council will have to approve the plans. Other groups that fall into this category would be any parish sub-committee or advisory group that oversees this area of parish life, such as the liturgy, evangelization, catechesis, and parish life committees. As every parish and diocese calls these committees by different names, and not every committee exists everywhere, you will have to decide which of the governing bodies in the parish have to approve your plan.

The unofficial categories are all of those people and groups in the parish who will be affected by the plan, those who are deeply entrenched in the parish fabric. In this category are the power groups in the parish, such as all the various historical men and women's groups (Holy Name, Knights, Altar Society, et al.) and all the groups connected to parish living (home/school, Mother's Club, Athletic Club, Over-60s, et al.). Failure to consult these groups could lead to failure. Actively consulting them could ensure your plan's success.

How to proceed

Getting "permits" from the official level usually follows a set pattern. You bring to them a proposal before you begin to plan, laying out an initial draft of your proposal, what you want to "build," how long it will take, an initial guess as to costs, and a far-stronger guess as to benefits. This initial formal process is the first step in the permit process: you can't start really putting your plan together until permission has been given to do so.

Once you have permission to proceed, clarify with the permission-granting groups when they want to see your plans as they develop. They may not want to see them again until you bring the final plans for its approval, or they may want to have regular monthly updates on how the plans are developing. If you report to a subcommittee of the parish council, then you will probably have to keep it informed on a monthly basis but then not speak to the whole council again until the final plans are in place.

Getting permits from the unofficial groups can be a lot more difficult and require a lot more work. Often it's best to have initial conversations with these groups early, before you are even sure what you are doing, to touch base with them. What do they think about how things are currently done in the parish? Any changes they'd like to see made or problems that need to be specifically addressed? Talking informally with these groups early is a great way to gather invaluable data about the parish, letting them know that you value their input, and getting their buy-in and support. As these groups' "permits" are informal, the process used to get their OK should be informal as well.

At issue here isn't what the process will be—every place will be different—but that you incorporate the approval process into your plans. Identify all the formal and informal permits you will need, determine the timetable in which they have to be gotten, and develop a strategy on how you will get the permits approved. Never go into a "permit" meeting without have a clear strategy in mind for getting approval. Always have prepared remarks at hand, along with answers to questions you expect to be asked. Know who the key persons are in the approval groups. You may want to approach them in advance about your proposal and seek their advice.

WILLINGNESS TO MODIFY

If your planning is to be successful, you must be willing to modify your plans along the way, whether because the powers-that-be want them changed or because you realize that they need to be adapted. Don't get locked into a particular way of doing things; be open to new possibilities as they come along.

Again, remember that these are not your plans. Others have the right and the duty to shape, adapt, and focus these plans so that they work in the best interest of the parish community. The more open you are to accepting input from others—no matter how critical it may be, no matter how it may change the shape of what you want to do—the more likely you will produce an effective plan. That doesn't mean that you make whatever change someone suggests, as it is suggested. Rather, take the advice as given and see how it can be incorporated into what you are trying to accomplish. Be open to advice; don't follow it blindly. While it isn't your plan, you have to own it.

No one else sees the vision you see; no one else has done the thinking you've done to establish the initial vision. Don't give it up too meekly; just don't hold on to it irrationally.

This raises an important point: what happens when your vision is changed completely during the permitting process? When the house you wanted to build by the lake is now a third-story walk-up condo in a sketchy part of town? If you've fought for your vision and can't make headway, you may have to step aside. It is very difficult to develop and implement a plan that you don't believe in. But you can also stay the course, winning whatever battles you can along the way to honor your beliefs. Whatever you choose in this situation won't be easy.

■ Discussion questions

▶ What is the value of the permit process in planning?

▶ Who are the formal groups from whom you will need permits? Who are the key people in these groups?

▶ Who are the informal groups from whom you will need permits? Who are the key people in these groups?

▶ When do you need to start getting these permits?

▶ What is your strategy for getting permits?

▶ How much time should you allow in your planning process in order to get all the necessary permits?

▶ What research do you need to prepare for the permit process?

▶ Who on the planning team will be responsible for getting all the permits?

Start at the beginning and work to the top
(Organization and implementation)

PREPARING TO BUILD

After the blueprints have been developed and approved and the permits secured, the physical work of building your house can start in earnest, although that doesn't mean that you can immediately start hammering nails or installing windows. There are initial steps that must be taken before any of the actual building can take place. These things include clearing the land and leveling it, putting in utilities and driveways, getting the footings dug and the foundation poured, and getting the necessary supplies ordered and delivered.

Your immediate response to this is probably, "Duh. I know that," and you probably do. Yet when I think back on all the horror stories I've heard about failed projects, I realize that many of the most crucial errors were made at this initial stage. People immediately want to jump to the stage where they can start seeing progress from their efforts. Planning processes most often fail because people reach this stage and immediately want to offer a program. As you begin this step in the planning process, understand one thing: you are not yet ready to choose a program. Only after completing this step will you have enough information to determine the number of different programs you will need, how and when you will use them to accomplish your mission, and the amount of resources that you will need for your plan to succeed as developed.

We're going to examine each element of methodical planning in order, a process that will work whether you are trying to set up an effective Bible study program, fundraising effort, or any other kind of parish initiative. We could easily call this part "Planning Out the Plan." Follow along with me.

PREPARING THE LAY OF THE LAND

If you've ever watched a building go up, I'm sure you noticed that the first thing that happens is surveyors arrive. They lay out the plot lines that mark the boundaries of the property. Then they lay out where the new building will be located on the property. They make exact measurements and mark where the foundation of the building will be placed. Then a bulldozer or other construction machinery comes on site and the ground is prepared for building: trees are felled, brush is cleared, and the contour of the land is shaped.

This basic prep work is rarely done in parish planning, but it's a crucial step. What needs to be done in your parish to prepare the land (the parishioners) in order to create an effective and successful program? While every parish is different, here are a few suggestions to consider. (I'm using a Bible study program here as an example, but again, this process applies to all kinds of parish planning.)

- What are people's attitudes about Bible study? Are they eager for it or lackadaisical? What types of promotional work will need to be done to whet people's appetite for the Bible study you want to offer? Will you need to put a series of items in the bulletin or begin with a series of presentations to get people engaged?
- What has been the history of Bible study in the parish in the past? Are there good memories or bad? How can you build upon the past programs or distance this program from a previous one that failed?
- Are there currently Bible study groups existing in the parish? How well are these known and accepted by parishioners? Will they be an asset or a liability to the Bible study you intend?

SETTING THE FOUNDATION

As Jesus says in the Gospel, a person who builds a house on sand is foolish. The wise person builds a house on rock, a solid foundation. That's true for your plan as well: It needs to be built on a solid foundation. So what's yours? What is the solid foundation on which you will build your Bible-centered church? Again, a series of questions:

- Does the parish already have a core group of people committed to studying and living the Scriptures? If so, how can you recruit them to your efforts? If not, is there a group of people who you can identify to form such a group? Regardless, such a group of committed people is essential if you are to achieve your goal. Part of your thinking should involve how you will identify, recruit, and prepare these leaders. You will need to develop strategies for accomplishing each of these steps.

- How will you prepare the parish for the planned initiative? You cannot take for granted that people will be interested in your plan, no matter how many surveys you conducted or data you gathered before putting your plan together. You will need a solid strategy for "selling" the plan to parishioners. Marketing always has two intended outcomes: (1) informing people of a product or an initiative and (2) helping them to see the benefits of using or participating in what is offered. So, what are your plans concerning a marketing campaign? How will you inform people about your initiative? What will you do to make them want to participate in it?

Marketing is both an art and a skill. If you are fortunate enough to have in your parish people who work in marketing campaigns, enlist their help. If you aren't so fortunate, then be sure to study successful marketing campaigns and borrow from them. McDonalds and other companies spend billions each year trying to inform and entice potential users of their products. Listen and watch what they do and learn from them. You don't need to launch an expensive print and e-media campaign, but you do need to inform potential clients and persuade them to participate in implementing your vision. Learn from the pros. See the Appendix for an outline of the essential elements in a successful marketing campaign.

Practically, you will want to establish a marketing committee. They will operate independently of the main planning committee but will be led by a member of the planning committee. Operating independently means being able to make decisions and act without unnecessary control. It doesn't mean they can do what they want: marketing campaigns need the approval of the planning committee along with the governing body—including the pastor—because what is actually being marketed here is the parish, not just a specific program. But once the marketing campaign is approved, the marketing committee should be left free to do its work. It will, of course, keep the planning committee informed of the work being done and what is being accomplished.

PUTTING IN THE INFRASTRUCTURE

When building a house the necessary infrastructure would be things like running electric, water, and sewer lines to your building site. In your parish project, this would be things such as communication networks—how you will register people, gather their data, and then use their data to contact them—scheduling events, and putting together leadership training for the folks who will coordinate and run the Bible initiative. Let's look at these a little more closely.

Communication Network If done correctly, the marketing campaign will generate interest in your plan. Do not equate interest with willingness to participate; interest means, "I'm curious. I'd like to know more. I'm willing to call for information." Be sure to provide a contact number for people to call if they are interested or if they want to register. Make sure the people staffing this contact number know how to answer the call. Give them a script of what to say on the phone to explain the program. Give them a spreadsheet so they can capture information from the caller so that follow-up calls and emails can be sent, in case they don't sign up immediately. Be sure that if people reach a voicemail message, their calls are returned within a few days—within twenty-four hours should be the standard. This means that you will need numerous people prepared to do the follow-up. How will you train these people?

ADDED BENEFITS OF A COMMUNICATIONS NETWORK

Your communication network will be an invaluable tool during the marketing and registration phase of your plan. It will be just as valuable from then on. Not only will this database serve as your base of information for all future projects—this becomes your "mailing" list to promote and advertise everything else you do—it also will be your conduit for passing along information and keeping people engaged throughout as you implement your plan. People are more likely to stay involved if they stay connected, and they will stay better connected the more they stay informed. So the marketing campaign shouldn't end when people are registered; it should continue throughout the entire plan. You will always want to recruit new people and encourage current participants to continue. The best marketing ammo you can get are the comments and stories of participants. Capture them regularly and share them widely.

Again, it would be valuable to have a group responsible for setting up the communication network and making sure it runs smoothly and effectively. A decision will need to be made by the pastor/parish council concerning how the data gathered is to be stored and used. Everyone involved in the process will need to be informed on the use of people's contact information, how it is to be handled securely, and how it is to be stored.

Training Here is a helpful rule of thumb for every activity you do: you will need one trained leader or facilitator for every eight to ten participants. These will be the people who facilitate discussion groups following a presentation on the Bible, people who will lead Bible study groups in their homes, or people who will facilitate Bible-centered prayer at various group sessions. You will need to identify the number of leaders you will need, determine how you will recruit them, and then, how you will prepare them for their roles. The training will be different for each leader, depending upon what he or she is being asked to do. A facilitator of discussion groups will need to know basic communication skills and how to run a group. A leader of a Bible study group will need preparation both in group leadership and communication skills, and formation in the Bible. The more training needed, the more time that must be allowed in advance for the preparation to occur.

If you plan to hold a Bible study program, make sure you schedule it at least six months in the future. This will not only allow you adequate time for marketing and registration, but it will also allow you time to prepare the number of leaders that you will need for their roles. Be aware that the success of your program will depend on the quality of these leaders. You cannot skimp on this stage of your plan.

COORDINATING EFFORTS

In most building projects of any size, you have two levels of contractors involved: general contractors and job contractors. Job contractors are responsible for various aspects of the building process. For example, I would hire an electrical contractor for the electrical part of the job, a plumbing contractor for water and sewer, and the like. The general contractor is the person or group who is responsible for the overall successful completion of the project. A similar arrangement is recommended for successful parish planning projects as well.

The overall planning committee will usually serve as the general contractor on its project—with the pastor and/or parish council serving as the owners, or final decision makers. The planning committee will then "job out" various aspects of the work to a subcommittee, a group formed by the planning committee to divide up the workload. Subcommittees need to be in constant contact with the planning committee—which is coordinating all the various groups working at the same time—but they also need to be able to work without constant management or interference. Appoint a group, give it its task along with any guidance you have, and then ask for regular reports. Other than that, let the appointed committee do its work.

Because the planning committee is responsible for oversight, it needs to keep well-informed about the work of the subcommittees. If it isn't happy with the work being done, speak up early: Don't be afraid to be hands-on if that is needed. One of the best ways of staying informed is to have a member of the planning committee serve as the head of each subcommittee. The planning committee member will, supposedly, be keenly aware of the planning committee's vision and will be able to keep the planning committee well-informed.

Everything in its own proper time

As much as we might want instant gratification, building a house or implementing a plan requires attention to detail and doing one step at a time—and in the proper order. That proper order is fairly easy to see when building a house—you know you can't put shingles on before the roof is built—but it is much more difficult to recognize in less concrete projects, such as helping your parish become more Bible-centered. More difficult, yes, but not impossible, as I've tried to show in this step. Take your time and identify all the steps that are needed to implement a successful plan. Do what is needed to prepare the land, put in the infrastructure, and build a solid foundation. If you do this, your chances of success improve greatly.

■ Discussion questions

▶ What are the obstacles that need to be cleared in your parish before a plan can be implemented? What strategies can you use to clear those obstacles aside?

▶ What infrastructure needs to be in place before you can implement your plan? What strategies will you use to install this infrastructure?

▶ Who are the key people who need to be part of the solid foundation for this plan? How will they be recruited and prepared for their role?

▶ How will you divide up the responsibilities for implementing your plan? How many subcommittees will you need? How will you keep informed about and oversee their work?

What can you afford?
(Finances)

I've intentionally avoided the topic of budgets and finances until now for a very particular reason: While budget issues must be addressed, asking budget questions too early in the planning process can short-circuit the process before the planning and visioning are complete. Finances should neither limit your vision nor determine what you accomplish. If you start by asking "How much will this cost?" then the budget automatically limits your dreaming. Practical questions will come up soon enough. So, dream first, and then worry about how you will pay for it.

The "Rule of Two of Three" applies to all projects, wherever they may occur. The rule states that there are three variables—speed, quality, and costs—and that you can only have two of those three at any one time. So if you want things done quickly, the project will either cost a lot more money or the quality will suffer. If you demand quality, the project will take longer to complete or will cost a lot more. And if you want to control costs, then projects are slowed down or the quality suffers.

Finances will determine (a) the speed at which you build, (b) how much you can accomplish at any given time, (c) your ability to use outside assistance, (d) the quality of materials you can choose. This means, simply, that if you don't have the money you need to accomplish everything you have in mind, you will need to do the project more slowly than you hoped, find ways of saving money along the way, and rely more on volunteers than paid personnel. For example, instead of a weekend, overnight retreat, you may have to settle for a one-day retreat. You get the idea.

An effective budgeting process

Once you have completed the previous steps in the planning process, you are now ready to begin the budgeting process. Go into this process well aware that unless someone wins the lottery and endows your project with untold riches, you won't have all the resources you need to accomplish everything in your plan immediately. That said, conduct the first step of the budgeting process with the same openness to the vision you have practiced throughout the planning process. Don't cut corners here; determine the resources you need to accomplish each step of your plan and write them down. For example:

- How much money will you need to blanket the area with ads? Include here costs for ad buys and mailing expenses.
- What will it cost to ensure that your marketing campaign reaches your desired audience? Include here IT costs for updating the website and sending out e-blasts.
- How many leaders do you want to train and how much will it cost to train them? Include here training resources, any outside assistance or program you plan to use, along with any hospitality costs you might have, such as babysitting, refreshments, a leader's retreat day.

- What will your expenses be to register participants and communicate with them? Include any additional phone and secretarial expenses, along with postage or related charges.
- Finally, figure in the cost of program materials—texts, videos, speaker stipends and expenses, etc.

Added together, all of these costs will give you the total amount you intend to spend in order to accomplish your plan. If your plan covers a number of years, make sure that you indicate that as well— show how your expenses will be spread out over the course of the next three to five years, or however long you think it will take to implement your plan.

Now that you know the proposed costs, you have to determine how you will pay for them. How much will be covered by fees charged to users? How much will be paid for by donations, fundraising events, and the like? How much will come from general parish funds? This all needs to be spelled out in your budget before you submit it for approval.

MAKING THE NUMBERS REALISTIC

Once you've put together the budget numbers based upon what you have planned, now—and not until now—is the time to look carefully at the budget and the plan side-by-side. The amount of money you can realistically expect to receive from parish funding, donations and fundraising, and user fees is the money you have to work with. Now, turn to the expense side of your budget and determine how you can best use this money to accomplish your goal. Where can you most effectively trim costs without seriously undermining your plan? What might you be able to put off until later in the process? Remember, you can control two of three variables. If you must control costs, do you sacrifice speed or quality? Do you put your money into producing the best programs and events over a longer period of time, or do you do the best you can with the money you have in the time you've allotted yourself?

A THOUGHT FOR BUDGETING...

One thing to keep in mind is the dynamics of group formation. If you've done your marketing well and sold people on the need for your plan, then you can expect very good turnout during the first year and possibly even your second year. This is when you begin to lose participants as people grow tired of the program, have changes to their lives that prevent their participation, or are eager to move to the next level on their own faith journey. So, income from fees will be less after year two until the next layer of your plan kicks in for those ready to make that leap.

GETTING THE BUDGET APPROVED

While you will want to keep your original budget as a touchstone, you submit the realistic budget for approval. As you did during the "permit" stage, be sure to have a strategy in place for getting your budget approved. Make sure you review the budget with the head of the finance committee and with the pastor before you submit it. Have people lined up to speak in favor of your budget. Be prepared to make adaptations to your budget where you can, and be prepared to fight for parts of the budget that you feel are the most important to its success. Make sure that you have a wonderful story to tell about how this plan will be beneficial to the parish. You've probably told this story many times during the permit phase; really sell it here. Be sure to add what the downsides are of not funding this plan: How will *not* funding it be detrimental to the parish?

As part of your story, make the case for investing in the future of the parish. For example, how will the parish benefit by having group leaders or facilitators trained? How might these people provide long-term service to the parish when they've finished participating in this particular plan? How might the formation provided as part of this plan lay the foundation for these trained leaders to become Lay Ecclesial Ministers or leaders of other parish groups or organizations? Make the case that you are preparing them for the future of the parish, not just so they can facilitate discussions or lead groups for a particular program. This is a valid argument. According to research, people who serve as Lay Ecclesial Ministers today had previously participated in leadership training provided by their parish as part of catechist formation or training for a particular program. So these training programs should be considered as long-term investments.

Also highlight the percentage of the budget that will come from fees and outside sources. Show how participants will be covering their own expenses and helping to pay for some of the organizational costs. Emphasize how much ownership the parish is already starting to take in the plan through its fundraising and other activities. Remember to make it clear that it isn't *your* plan that you seek to fund, but the *parish's* plan for growing as a community of faith.

CONCLUSION

Budgets are realities that we all face, but lack of money should never stop us from planning effectively. We just have to figure out ways of using our money wisely. The ironic thing about a systemic planning process is that you may well spend less money than you would on an episodic approach: Because you've thought through all of the steps that you need to take and have a good idea what each will cost, you won't continually be coming back to the well seeking additional funding for the next new program or event. Because of your plan, the parish will have a clear idea of what its expenses will be in this area for the next few years, so it too can budget effectively.

Systemic planning can also help you make a stronger case for the money you need. Because you have thought your process through thoroughly, you can show what you will be accomplishing at each step in the process and how money invested in your programming will lead to stronger outcomes. As you implement your plan successfully, you may receive more money because finance folks are more likely to give support to leaders who can show a return on the investment.

■ Discussion questions

▶ Which of the three elements—cost, speed, quality—is most important to the success of your plan? Which are you most willing to sacrifice in order to accomplish your plan?

▶ What is your response to the following statements? "Participants should pay all expenses related to any program that benefits them personally." "The parish should pay all expenses for programs that benefit the parish, whether directly or indirectly."

▶ How will implementing your plan benefit the parish? How will not implementing the plan harm the parish?

▶ What percentage of the parish do you expect to participate in your plan during the first year? second year? third year? How does your budget reflect these numbers of participants?

▶ What is your strategy for getting your budget approved? What is your strategy for fundraising and donations? How will you determine the cost of any programming you intend to offer?

STEP 7

Use the right tools for the job
(Programs)

Anyone who has been involved in ministry for any length of time can tell stories about the time when they heard about the fabulous success another parish or diocese was having with a program. Like wildfire, news of these wonderful "silver bullets" or "magic beans" spread from bishop to bishop, pastor to pastor, superintendent to superintendent, diocesan director to diocesan director, principal to principal, or parish catechetical leader to parish catechetical leader. The message spread always goes something like this: "We are using this program and you wouldn't believe the results we've been getting—people are actively participating in the program, they are returning to Mass in droves, and our collections are up by 130%."

Wow! Which bishop, pastor, or school or ministerial leaders wouldn't want these amazing results? And because you've heard about the program from a friend and equal in ministry, a great deal of trust already exists in the goodness of the product, so it's likely that you won't give it the due diligence you normally would if someone you didn't know tried to sell you the program out of the blue. So, based upon your friend's recommendation, you immediately order the program, scope it out quickly to get a grasp of how to use it, and then rapidly implement it in your parish or ministry. Why not, if you can get such amazing results with so little effort? It would almost seem like a dereliction of duty if you didn't hop on board the bandwagon, right?

The problem, of course, is that just adopting a program is not always in the best interest of the end user. What's missing from the word-of-mouth advertising are all the steps the original parish or diocese took when it began the program. Remember these questions: What was the original user's vision and mission? What were they trying to accomplish with the program? How did they fit the program to their parishioners? How did they lay a solid foundation and prepare the necessary infrastructure in order for the program to succeed?

Bottom line: There are no silver bullets or magic beans. What is required for a program to succeed is a clear vision, knowledge of and how to work with a specific community, a well-thought-through blueprint that lays out each step that must be taken and when it must be taken, the finances needed to implement the plan in an appropriate amount of time, and the right tools for the job—a resource designed to accomplish what you want to accomplish in this phase of the journey—and a lot of hard work!

WHERE DID WE GO WRONG?

Another blind spot many parishes or ministries have is that they tend to think that they need only one program, and all will be well if they simply implement that program correctly. Such thinking leads people to think that "doing" the program is itself the goal, when at best it is merely a strategy that one uses to accomplish a particular goal. Remember that accomplishing a goal is, in itself, not an intended outcome; accomplishing a goal is, at best, merely a strategic step in achieving the mission. The mission is what is important. The mission is why we do what we do; all else are just the means we use to accomplish that end. Remember the phrase related to social justice: think globally; act locally? Well, that is a statement that also relates to the planning process. Keep the global (mission) always in your sights because that's where you want to end up. Working locally (accomplishing goals and objectives) means taking the steps needed to complete the journey.

KNOW YOUR TOOLS

Just as you need many different types of tools in order to build a house, you will need many different types of programs, processes, and procedures in order to implement your plan successfully. It is good to keep in mind that each tool is designed to accomplish a specific task or tasks. In the case of a parish, such tools would include textbooks, renewal programs, stewardship efforts, or Small Christian Community projects. No one program is the solution to a problem; each one is only a means you can use to help you to accomplish a particular task.

If a program is going to work properly, it has to be the proper program for the job that needs to be accomplished. This means that you should study a program to see what it is designed to accomplish and then see how well it matches with what you are trying to accomplish. This also means that you shouldn't try to make programs do what they weren't designed to do. Just as you wouldn't use a hammer to cut boards, you wouldn't use a program designed for adults with second graders.

It makes no difference what the project is, whether pulling nails from salvaged lumber, putting up billion-dollar buildings, or improving the evangelization process in your parish, it is important that you understand the job fully, choose the proper tool or tools needed to accomplish the task at hand, and use the tool fully and as it was designed until the job is finished, if you expect to get maximum results from your labors. Don't use the wrong tool for the job and don't give up on a tool just because it doesn't work as fast as you want it to work. Give up on it only when you are sure that it wasn't the right tool to use.

CHOOSING THE PROPER TOOL FOR THE JOB

As suggested above, one of the major reasons why plans don't succeed is that the program—the tool—chosen to implement the plan undermines it. It's not that the program is flawed. The problem is that people are trying to use one program to accomplish multiple jobs. Instead of asking, "What program do I need to help me accomplish this task?" ask, "What *programs* do I need?"

Because you are planning systemically, you are not simply looking to run a program or accomplish a task. No, you now have a detailed plan in place for how you are going to accomplish your mission. Looking at your written plans and knowing what you have to accomplish first in order to lay a solid foundation for everything else that follows, you will then recognize that you have numerous jobs that have to be done. You've broken these out into easily achievable segments, and now you have to choose the right tools for the jobs you want to accomplish. One program may be enough—like a Swiss Army knife, it might be able address numerous different functions—but you may need several. Recognizing this fact alone will save you lots of time and energy.

I'm not proficient with my hands. I'm what my brothers who work in construction call a "jack-legged" carpenter. I can get the job done but it may take me five times as long to accomplish, and the finished product will lack the polish of a professional job. One of the reasons a task takes me so long to accomplish is that I'm always going back to the toolbox for tools I didn't realize I would need. My brothers don't have this problem. They examine the task at hand and think it through in their minds before ever picking up a tool. They know exactly what needs to be done and what tools they will need to use to accomplish the task well. They make sure they have those tools handy and ready to use even before they leave the shop.

Apply this same foresight—what Senge in *The Fifth Discipline* calls "mental modeling"—to all of your plans. Before starting on a particular task, work it through in your mind. How long do you think it will take? How much help will you need? What unexpected problems might you encounter? You've already accounted for costs in your budgeting process. Here you want to ask the questions, "Do I have enough resources for the job or will I need more? If more, where will I get them?" (No one ever complained when a job cost less or took less time than budgeted. Thinking through the steps of the job before beginning may well save you both!)

Once you've thought through the job at hand, now you can begin to choose the proper tools.

Start by clearly naming what it is you want to accomplish at this particular stage in a task. Let's say that your overall mission is to improve the quality of how liturgy is celebrated in your parish and you've determined that the first place you want to start is by improving how your current lectors proclaim the readings. You've decided that your approach here will have three components: (1) training the lectors on proclamation skills—stance, projection, enunciation, clarity, timing, tonality, and putting emotion appropriately into their reading; (2) teaching the lectors preparation skills, simple practice routines that they can use to prepare for each reading; (3) helping the lectors grow in their own personal understanding and love for the Scripture they are called to proclaim.

Once you have determined the *what*, spend some time identifying the *how*: What procedures are needed to accomplish these three tasks? How long will each take to complete? What is your deadline for getting this done? Can you handle all three elements at once or will you need to break these into three separate tasks? What resources (programs, tools) are available to help you accomplish these tasks? What will these cost? What training is needed to use them? Is there anyone qualified to use them or will someone need to be sent for training? What is your budget?

Now, you are ready to choose and implement your training program. Set up a time schedule, and advertise the event, being sure to explain why it is needed, what it is designed to accomplish, and the benefits to the individual and to the parish for taking part in this training. Be sure to emphasize that this is the first stage of an overall parish effort to make liturgy more worshipful and meaningful for all.

Taking your time, doing it right the first time

People are amazingly patient. They will put up with sporadic fits and starts, misguided efforts, and utter foolishness for far longer than one would think possible. They will also become amazingly impatient over the seemingly least important things. That being said, the rule is *don't test people's patience unnecessarily*. Take your time in choosing a program so that you only have to do it once. Once doesn't mean that you will never have to do another program or that additional training won't be needed—more on this in the chapter on evaluation. Once means, we've set our direction, we know what we are doing, this is the way we are going, and we don't plan to make major changes to it for some time.

Once you've started, give your plans time to work. If you've put a program in place that you know will take a year to be successful, give it a year to be successful. That doesn't mean that you can't make changes to how the program is implemented or make minor adjustments along the way—again, see Evaluation for more on this—it means that you aren't going to bail at the first hint of trouble or dissatisfaction that the program isn't working better or faster. If you've done your homework on the program, you have a good idea of what to expect, how people will respond, and what adaptations you might need to make.

If you need to see results faster than a particular program is designed to deliver them, but you also value the overall results the program is designed to deliver, then supplement the one program with other activities and trainings. No matter how good a program is, no one program can accommodate every facet of an issue.

CLOSING THOUGHTS

Programs are wonderful tools. Like this book, they represent the thinking and practice of experienced and professional trainers captured in a way that they can help you accomplish desired tasks. As long as you remember that programs are designed to accomplish particular tasks only and not every task, you will be ready to go.

Remember, too, that choosing the proper program takes time and effort on your part, just as the implementation of the program will require time and effort. Be prepared to make that effort and to allow for that time in your planning.

■ Discussion questions

▶ What is your attitude about programs in general?

▶ How have you used programs in the past? How well have they worked? What have you accomplished with them? How satisfied or disappointed have you been with the programs you've used?

▶ After reading this chapter, how have your attitudes about using programs changed or been affected?

How are you doing?
(Evaluation)

Evaluations are very important in any process, whether related to planning or not. They help you determine:

- what has been accomplished,
- how well you have accomplished what you set out to accomplish,
- what more needs to be done before you can be satisfied, and
- whether or not what you are doing is actually helping you to accomplish what you set out to accomplish.

I will examine each of these areas in more detail in the rest of this chapter. Here I will simply say that an effective evaluation process needs to be an essential component of every planning process, at every step of the way. If not, you have no way of measuring the success of what you are doing, whether you are even on the right road to accomplish you mission, or what you need to do to get back on track.

In this chapter I intend to teach you how to think about evaluation, how to evaluate effectively at each step of any process, planning or otherwise, and show you how to determine effective criteria to use to create effective evaluation questions. You might even learn to write questions that elicit the responses you want and need, but I can't promise that. When you finish this chapter, I invite you to evaluate how well or how poorly I accomplished what I've said I'm going to accomplish. I'll provide a set of evaluation questions you can use to evaluate this chapter and this book. I'll even provide my email address so you can send your evaluations to me if you'd like. The only way I'm going to improve my work is if I'm willing to hear from you on the effectiveness of what I am doing.

THE PURPOSE OF EVALUATION

The first purpose of evaluation is to collect usable data, data that you can analyze to help you learn what you've accomplished and how well you've accomplished it, and how much more work you need to do to accomplish this stage of the plan.

Objective evaluation is difficult and time-consuming in church work, much more so than in building our dream house, for example. But this means that the process you use to collect the data and analyze it is that much more important. Just as you can't take the next step in the building process before the previous dependent step is finished, you can't take the next step in your plan until the first step is done to a necessary level of satisfaction. This means that you have to know what your criteria for success are at every level. When you look at a freshly laid tile floor you don't want to see bumps and cracks and discolored tiles. You know what a successfully laid floor should look like. You need to determine that same level of desired outcome for every step of your plan.

THE FOUR LEVELS OF EVALUATION

Over the years I've participated in countless evaluations, read the responses from the people who have taken the evaluations, and tried to make sense of the messages they were trying to send. I've read and lamented the poor quality of survey questions and processes that are frequently used, and become very disappointed that we as a church seem incapable of developing effective evaluative instruments. (See the Appendix for examples of unsatisfactory evaluation questions.)

Over time I have come to realize that there are four distinct levels that have to be a part of every evaluation process. Those levels are identified by the following questions:

1. What did we do and how well did we do it?
2. How well did we accomplish what we set out to accomplish?
3. Have we accomplished all we need to do here before moving forward or is there more work that still needs to be done?
4. Is what we are doing accomplishing what we want it to accomplish or are we going in the wrong direction?

Let's look at each of these four "levels" individually to understand them fully. Before I do that though, please note that I call these *levels*, not steps. The intent of this is to help you recognize that you don't do one, and then the next, and so on. No, what has to happen is that after the first level, the collection of usable data, you have to spend time analyzing and digesting what you've collected. Just as the first level is engaged in collecting data, the next three levels are designed to help you analyze that data to get the most out of it.

1. What did we do and how well did we do it? While these are seemingly simple questions, how you answer them tells a lot about your planning process. It isn't uncommon to hear people comment,

"What did we do? Well, we held the workshop, didn't we? How well did we do? Well, we had fifteen people show up." Such answers, while factual, aren't very helpful. The purpose of this level of the evaluation is to help you to collect the data you will need to assess the effectiveness of your plan and to help you to make any corrections you may need to make early on.

You have a plan. You know what you are trying to do at this stage in your plan. Perhaps you are trying to train lectors or catechists. You have several steps in the training process, and let's say this is the first one. You've set initial goals for this session: participants will learn that the Bible is divided into Old and New Testaments, that there are a variety of different books in the Bible, and they will learn to find passages in the Bible. These are your immediate goals: simple, clear, and straightforward. What you want to do in this level of the evaluation process is to ask questions to determine what people learned in these three areas and how well they learned it. You are seeking factual knowledge—can they find a passage in the Old or New Testament?—as well as comprehension knowledge—do they understand it?

Before you can do this, you have to set your learning and comprehension goals before any event begins. By knowing what you want to accomplish in any given event, you not only guarantee that the event will go more smoothly and be better accepted, you will also be able to better measure just how well you accomplished these goals. These goals become criteria you will use to write your evaluation questions. Also, having an idea of what data you will need in order to assess the plan's success will help you to ask better data-gathering questions.

There is a secret to creating and conducting surveys that marketing folks know. I don't have space here—or the knowledge—to go into this in great detail. So, if you need help conducting surveys, my advice to you is to look for people in your parish who conduct surveys for a living and ask them to give you a hand. Most of them are more than willing to help. If you don't, check online for articles that discuss creating effective surveys. You'll find lots of information there that will help you develop better survey instruments and teach you how to conduct an effective survey that yields good data.

Evaluations should be short and sweet. While it is always best to collect evaluations from everyone immediately following an event, getting people to take the time to fill out a decent-length evaluation immediately will often prove impossible. So don't be afraid to use social media. Send an email out to all participants following an event and ask for their evaluation. You can also send it out to a few randomly selected participants and get possibly even better results, depending in each on how many responses you receive. From a sociological perspective, you are more likely to get a usable response back from a group if only a third is invited to fill out a survey, if they have been prepared to receive it, and if they are asked politely to fill it in and return it in a few days. Get it to them quickly and give them a reasonable but not excessive time limit to complete it, and you will get them back.

To summarize, at this level you are looking to collect data that you can use at later levels to assess the effectiveness of both your plan and this particular program that you are using to implement your plan. Everything else is extraneous.

2. How well did we accomplish what we set out to accomplish? At this level you begin the process of data analysis. This isn't too complex or difficult. You just want to judge from the data how well you accomplished your immediate goals for this event.

Far too often it seems that people haven't set success criteria for the various stages of the plans they develop or the programs they offer to implement those plans. So when asked, "How well did you accomplish what you set out to accomplish?" they may well answer, "Well, we held the parent sac prep program and all the parents showed up." If pushed a bit they may add, "They left happy, they seemed to enjoy the movie, and they seem energized for the year ahead."

But for people seeking to implement a systemic plan, such answers won't be acceptable. Systemic planners will have set success criteria for each goal and each objective identified in their plan. For them, a successful parent program might have the following goals and objectives:

Goal: That the parents of children receiving First Communion be prepared to actively share their love for Christ and the Church, and their devotion to the Eucharist, with their children.

Objectives:
- Help parents name and talk about their own faith journey.
- Help parents understand how their attitudes and participation at Mass shape the attitudes and participation of their children.
- Help parents develop and agree to implement at home at least three daily rituals designed to promote faith in Jesus and the Church.
- Get parents excited about the role they will play in the coming year's preparation before reception of the Blessed Sacrament.
- Answer parents' questions.

The well-planned program will then have identified strategies on how each of these items will be accomplished.

These objectives and strategies define your success criteria. You know that you have been totally successful if you have accomplished all of them well. It's OK if you achieve some things and not others; you may have attempted to do too much in one setting and may have to offer another session to do it all well. During the session you may realize that the parents need more training than you can provide them in one session. That's more data for analysis.

You will have used these criteria to help you develop your survey questions used at the data-collection level. Here, you begin to unpack that data to understand how well you accomplished your objectives. So, what kind of data do you need?

Well, you need data that shows whether or not your parents could name and talk about their own faith journey. Do they understand that their attitudes and participation at Mass shape the attitudes and participation of their children? Did they agree to implement at least three daily rituals at home to promote faith in Jesus and the Church? Are parents excited about the role they will play in the coming year's preparation? Were parents' questions answered? So, when you collect data, you must ask questions designed to get answers to these questions. I'll address this more fully below.

Once you have this data, read it carefully. You might find it helpful to group all the answers to each question separately so you can examine people's responses collectively. This will quickly give you a general idea of how successful you were. This will also let you see where some parents might be more engaged than others.

Don't go crazy here. This isn't rocket science. Look at the data you collected, see what it says, and understand what you've accomplished. Now you are ready to move to the next level in the process.

3. Have we accomplished all we need to do here before moving forward or is there more work that still needs to be done? Remember, holding that parent First Eucharist session was not your goal. The goal here is that parents become more active participants in the faith formation of their children. This parent session is a strategy used to accomplish one of your objectives. Because you have named this clearly in your plan, you know that you have several other objectives to meet in preparing parents to take on their important role. So what you want to know now is, have the parents been prepared? With what you've done with them in this meeting, can you now turn them loose on their own to work with the children at home with little guidance from you? If you can, great, because now you can move on to the next step of the plan. If you can't, you need to know this, because the rest of your plan depends on parent participation. If parents aren't ready yet to take on this responsibility, what additional training might they need to get there? Those are the types of questions you need to answer at this level.

Again, this doesn't need to be too difficult or complex. Simply study the information you've gathered and determine whether you are satisfied with what's been done. If parents have actively participated in the session, if they've energetically shared their faith with another person, if they have willingly created their three action steps, if they've asked a lot of good questions about their roles, then you have all the evidence you need to move forward. But if you got different responses for many of these items, if more than one or two parents have been reluctant to participate or get engaged, then you know that more work needs to be done to prepare them.

Again, don't get bogged down here. The purpose of this level is simply to check your progress. Once you know that, move quickly to the next level.

4. Is what we are doing accomplishing what we want it to accomplish or are we going in the wrong direction? In *The Fifth Discipline,* Senge offers a definition for burnout. Using Blessed Teresa of Calcutta as an example, Senge maintains that burnout is not caused by over-work. He argues that what causes burnout is inner tension: What you are doing is not accomplishing what you want to accomplish. Working to counter-purposes causes frustration, anger, and eventu-ally burnout—"I quit. I can't take this any more."

That's why this final level of evaluation is important. What you want to do is simply look at the data you collected, look at what you have accomplished, and simply ask, "Is this helping us to accom-plish our goal?" If you can answer yes, then move to the next step. If the answer is "no" or "not sure," then take a little more time to think about what you are doing and why. What would need to change in order to get the results you desire? Is a change of focus or approach necessary?

Again, this is not meant to be too difficult or complex. Simply take the time to make sure that your efforts are in tune with your goals. The maxim is "Work smarter, not harder," and that's what this level of evaluation helps you do.

CRITERIA TO USE TO DEVELOP EVALUATION QUESTIONS

As previously mentioned, evaluation questions should normally flow from your goals and objectives. The more specific you are in setting goals and objectives, the easier it will be to use these to set success criteria.

Let's look at a few examples, continuing to use engaging parents in their child's sacramental preparation as our model. Say that one of your objectives reads, "Parents will learn how to share their faith with their children." The success criteria here is that every parent will be able to demonstrate the ability to speak openly about their faith with their child. Here's the question: What happens if fifty percent of parents can do this and fifty percent can't? Is this a success or not? So your success criteria have to be different from your goals and objectives. Perhaps your success criterion is that most parents can do this well, some can do it a bit, and fewer than twenty percent struggle with the task.

Or say that your objective is that "parents can lead their children in praying before meals." Your success criterion could be that every parent has a copy of the before meal prayer and has prayed that prayer at least once.

Again, don't get caught up in wording; that's relatively unimportant. What is important is that you establish success criteria for each step in your plan. How will you know when the plan has been successful? That's what the criteria will help you to determine. In addition, by setting these criteria before you begin, you will better shape what you do so that your efforts are focused on accomplishing outcomes, not just holding a meeting. Never, ever, hold a meeting, a presentation, or a program without first naming at least a few things that have to be accomplished during this event.

How to conduct effective evaluations

As I've previously mentioned, there is both an art and a science to creating and evaluating surveys. You will be well served if you have someone on your planning team who works in this field, as that person can help you to collect the best data. If you don't have someone, then my comments below should be helpful.

The most effective way to collect data is to simply ask people. Randomly choose about ten percent of your group and invite their responses to a couple of questions. Using the last example, ask the parents, "How comfortable do you feel sharing your faith with your child?" or "How confident do you feel saying grace with your child before meals?" If you want, ask people to rate themselves on a scale from one to five, with one being "low confidence" or "uncomfortable" and five being "highly confident" or "very comfortable." You can then ask a follow-up question, such as "Why do you feel this way?" The final question would be, "What more help do you need to become comfortable (or confident)?"

These are the basic questions that should be asked for each of your success criteria. Keep the number of questions limited; this personal interview must be able to be conducted quickly. If you need to ask more than six questions, then you need to go to a written evaluation instrument. Whether written or oral, the questions you ask should be the same, focused on getting data to help you evaluate the success of your efforts.

If you have enough questions to warrant a written evaluation, there are many ways you can do this. These can be done on paper, you can set up an evaluation form on your parish website, or you can set up an account with a company that allows you to develop survey instruments online and then have people go online to take the evaluation. The website will record all data and provide it to you. If you set up questions that will allow for rating-scale answers (one to five), the online tool will also tabulate the data—doing the Math for you—and provide you with results. I'm most familiar with Survey Monkey (www.surveymonkey.com) but there are many other similar sites on the web.

These sites have made collecting and tabulating data so much easier to do that I highly recommend them to you. But whether you are conducting the survey orally, using pen and paper, or online, remember: If you don't ask good questions, you will not get good data. It is as simple as that. That's why I continue to focus on the importance of your questions. I'd also highly recommend that you field-test your questions with a few people before asking them formally. You want to make sure the questions can be understood—and understood in the way you want them understood—and quickly answered. For most local evaluations, simply ask one or two people not involved in the session to read them for clarity. See what kind of answers they will give you as well. Here are a few other suggestions:

- Avoid questions that lead people to a particular answer or show a bias, such as "Don't you agree that we should pave the parking lot first before painting the church?"

- Keep questions simple and focused on one thing only. A well-written question would be, "How satisfied are you with the quality of the cantors at the 5 PM Saturday Mass?" or "Do you prefer the music at 5 PM on Saturday or the choir at 11?" but never try to address two issues in one question— "How satisfied are you with the quality of the cantors and lectors at the 5 PM Saturday Mass?" unless you provide separate answer spaces for each. It is still better to ask each question separately.

- Avoid questions that can be answered with "yes," "no," or "who cares," unless you simply want to collect numerical data. So "Do you attend 5 PM Mass regularly?" would be fine if you want to know how many people attend this Mass or if you want to only get answers from people who attend this Mass. It isn't very helpful if you are trying to understand why people attend this Mass or what they think about it.

- Limit the number of questions so that people can complete the survey instrument in five minutes or less. People generally like to be asked their opinion, but they don't want to waste a lot of time in doing it. Get in, get what you need, and get out. Regularly offered surveys offered frequently generally collect more usable data than long surveys asked once.

Part of the science surrounding data collection is in developing the best questions and part is in choosing the right people to answer them. The best data is that collected from everyone: you have thirty parents in the first Eucharist class and you receive answers from all thirty. You can't get any better than that. But what if you have thirty, and only twenty reply? Is the data collected valid and can it be trusted? Sure, but it will raise questions, such as "Why didn't the other ten people respond?" Is this a case where the unheard-from ten don't care? This is why randomly choosing people to respond is often the best approach. Generally speaking, data collected randomly is just as valid as data collected from partial groups, and may be more so. Randomness keeps you from stacking the deck, asking only those people whom you know like what you were doing. Choosing randomly avoids this problem.

EVALUATING THIS WORK

I promised you an opportunity to evaluate this book, so here it is. Using what you've learned about the evaluation process, answer the following questions. In order to do this you need to know that my success criteria were (1) Help the readers gain an understanding of systemic planning, (2) Help the readers learn enough about systemic planning to be able to plan more effectively, and (3) Provide the readers with the tools they need to plan more effectively.

- What is systemic planning and why is it a valuable idea to consider?

- What are the benefits of systemic planning over episodic planning? What are its shortcomings?
- On a scale of one to five, with one being low and five being high, how comfortable are you with attempting to plan systemically?
- What additional information or help do you need to become more comfortable?
- What additional tools do you need in order to plan more effectively?

I welcome your answers to these questions and any feedback you might care to offer to improve the planning process. Please send this information to the following email address: mulhallpc@yahoo.com.

■ Discussion questions

- ▶ From reading this chapter, what are three key things you've learned about the importance of evaluation?
- ▶ From reading this chapter, what are three key things you've learned about the purpose of evaluation?
- ▶ From reading this chapter, what are three key things you've learned about the process of evaluation?
- ▶ What is your attitude about evaluations?
- ▶ How is the process described here different or similar to the process you've used in the past?
- ▶ What additional information do you need to evaluate more effectively?

Conclusion

Throughout this book I've provided you with a step-by-step way of thinking about the planning process. I have not tried to teach you an unfailing way to plan successfully, because there isn't one. Neither is there one guaranteed plan for success—all planning methods can be successful and all can fail; there are no guarantees.

My hope is that this book has provided you with ideas that will improve the success of your planning processes. Ultimately though, any success you experience will be because of the work that you do. Best wishes. Be not afraid.

Case studies pro and con

I. Episodic vs. systemic planning

St. Mildred's has a very large sacramental preparation program during the first and second grade years. They have more than 3,000 young people participating in religion classes (most of whom also receive the sacraments of Penance and Eucharist), and close to 1,200 parents participating in the mandatory parent programming connected to the sacraments—if they don't come, their children don't receive the sacraments. The pastor, DRE, and pastoral council are all equally delighted with the numbers of people participating in this phase of the parish's catechetical programming and with what the children and parents are being taught. However, once you move to the later years of the program the numbers don't look so good. In fact, there are more children in grades one and two classes than there are in the next six years combined. This does not look good on diocesan reports, and the pastor is getting calls from the bishop about fixing the prob-

lem. You've been asked by the pastor to serve on a committee to find out why so few children return after receiving the sacraments and, correspondingly, why so few of the families of these children actively participate in parish activities or even attend Sunday Mass regularly. Where do you begin?

If you are operating out of an episodic planning model, you will probably start by examining the parish instructional program to find out what is being done wrong. You'd probably speak to a random sample of the parents—and if you are really astute, to a random sample of the children as well—to find out what they did and didn't like about the program, and why they don't participate in religious education or Sunday Mass. You'd probably also sit in on some sessions to evaluate what is being done, and meet with the teachers and planners to hear what they thought about the program. The answers you'd gather would allow you to make a recommendation to the pastor to make a few changes in the program, such as adding an extra parent session to impress upon the parents in the most influential way you can the importance of their ongoing participation in the regular religion classes and Sunday Mass. This approach might work for a while, but it won't be long before the problem is again just as bad as it is now. What do you do next?

This type of case is not an isolated one. Far from it—it is the reality in almost every parish in the United States. I know this because I've worked in the religion textbook publishing business, and sales figures don't lie. If charted on a graph, the situation would look like this: first and second grade numbers were on a high plateau, numbers for third through fifth grade looked like a gradual ski slope, and six through eighth grade looked like they fell off of the table. The only variable to this was when the sacrament of confirmation was held during one of these elementary years.

So, what's the problem? To be sure, I'd have to carry out the type of investigation that I suggested above to gather as much information about the current program as I could. I'd talk with parents and children, I'd investigate the quality of the classes, and I'd talk with the teachers and the program planners. That would give me hard data to analyze. But approaching this problem as a systemic planner, I would also ask a different set of questions and seek different types of answers. For example, I'd ask the program planners, "What results are you seeing from your programs? What results are you trying to accomplish? How is this program designed to lead to a lifetime's participation in the sacraments of Penance and Eucharist? How is the program designed to help the parents become better parents and the family a more loving and religious family? How is it designed to get parents actively engaged in the lives of their children and in the life of the parish community?" I'd ask similar questions of the parents and children. I'd also ask similar questions of the pastor and the pastoral council, two groups that probably wouldn't be interviewed in the first scenario.

The questions an episodic planner might ask would focus on what is being done and how it is being done, and its effectiveness would be measured by the number of participants who take part in the process and the number of people who receive the sacraments. The systemic planner might ask questions concerned more with what people were trying to accomplish by what they were doing. Once these questions were answered, the investigation would try to determine what was actually being accomplished. Finally, the systemic planner would seek to judge the effectiveness of what was being done based upon how well the program was accomplishing its intended outcomes, recognizing, of course, that the intended outcomes might not be broad enough and so might need to be changed.

Here's what I think is wrong with the program at St. Mildred's (and at all of the other programs across the country that St. Mildred's represents): the focus is on receiving First Communion and First Penance and not on preparing children for lifelong sacramental participation. The sacraments are too often the carrot that's held out to the parents, and not allowing children to receive the sacraments is the stick that's used to force most parents to participate in the parent sessions. And we wonder why the majority of families often don't return to a formation program or possibly even to Mass, until the next big ritual event, confirmation, occurs. I'm surprised more people don't walk away and never come back. They've gotten the only thing that our approach says is important, the sacraments of Penance and Eucharist. Yes, I know that we tell them with words about all of the important reasons for coming back, but that's not what we tell them with our actions and emphasis. I believe that we emphasize the first reception of the sacraments so much that people can hear nothing else. So, from a systemic planner's perspective, if I were asked to fix the problem of people not participating in parish life much after second grade, the first place I'd look to fix would be the "successful" sacramental preparation part of the program.

Addendum to Chapter 1: Getting started

Why is forming leaders important? Forming parish catechists is a perfect example of this, as would be forming parish leaders. There will never be a time when this type of formation won't be needed; it will always be a strategy during every planning cycle. Why? Because catechists or parish leaders move, their lives or jobs change, they need a break, or your program is so successful that you continually need additional new catechists or leaders to staff it. So if leadership formation is what you are trying to accomplish, you'll never finish the task. But you can ask questions such as these: "What do you want these catechists or leaders to accomplish? How might we prepare them differently so that they are better prepared to achieve our desired outcomes?" Once you answer those types of questions you've opened up a doorway into a different way of addressing the problem. Now you are aiming for a prize bigger than preparing generic leaders: you are now preparing leaders who can make your programming more effective, your parish a better place to belong. Do you begin to see why systemic planning is important?

ADDENDUM TO CHAPTER 6, STEP 5: WHAT MAKES A MARKETING PLAN WORK?

From the reactions I hear at workshops, most parish promotional campaigns seem heavy on information and invitation, but light on benefits. They tell people about the who, what, when, where, and why of an event or initiative—usually very light on the why—but fail to explain the significance and benefits of what is being done. A successful marketing campaign will sell both the sizzle and the steak: it will share the vision of the planning team and the practical information people need to make a decision.

A successful marketing campaign will include informational and promotional ads that are widely distributed around the parish and the surrounding areas. Besides the bulletin and the parish website, consider including them in regular email blasts to parishioners and posting the ads in diocesan and local newspapers, and in community service announcements on local TV and radio outlets. While each ad should contain the essential information—especially about how to register—they should also be different in style and makeup. I might ignore one style of an ad and be captivated by another. So vary the ads each time they run.

But don't limit your marketing campaign to ads. The marketing campaign has to make people *want* what you have to offer. People have many other ways of spending their limited time. Why should they spend it with you and at this program? Develop a persuasive argument and present it in creative ways.

- Enlist the efforts of members of your parish who are already deeply engaged in Scripture study. Have them write short essays or tell brief stories of how their lives have been changed for the better by spending time with the Bible.
- Enlist the help of people in the parish to develop a series of videos capturing these people's comments.
- Start a "whispering" campaign to get people talking about the "something new" that is coming.
- Put together a speaker's bureau that can visit every parish group and organization to talk up the benefits of the parish's efforts to become a more Scripture-based community.

These are just a few ideas to seed your marketing process. Feel free to use them, but also be sure to come up with new ideas of your own.

ADDENDUM TO CHAPTER 9, STEP 8: WHAT EVALUATIONS ARE NOT

Does this ever happen to you? You spend the night in a hotel or you purchase a new pair of shoes, and the next thing you know, you are receiving emails from the company asking you to evaluate the quality of service and the merchandise you just bought. Most of the time I get the impression that the company couldn't care less about what my actual experience was. All they really seem to want is my praise: If they get rated less than perfect on an evaluation, then there is hell to pay at the corporate office. I've even had a car dealer call me and beg me to change an answer on a question because if I didn't, the dealership wouldn't qualify for a bonus from the manufacturer.

Using evaluations in this way makes them a joke. Unfortunately, most evaluations that I've seen used in parishes aren't a lot better. They often ask such silly things as "Rate the speaker on a scale of one to ten, with one low and ten high." This is a silly question because you are not asking the participant to rate the speaker on any particular item. So, if I think the speaker dresses and talks funny, should I give him a one? If the speaker has made me laugh the entire evening but I didn't learn anything from him, should I give her a ten? What are the criteria to be used in rating the speaker? Was he lively and entertaining? Did I learn something new? These questions all go begging here.

And the questions never seem to get any better. Do any of these look familiar?

- Please rate the quality of handout or visuals.
- Please rate your satisfaction with the evening.
- Please rate the length of breaks (!).
- Please rate the quality of refreshments.
- Please rate the quality of the meeting room.

All of these questions, and many much worse ones, appear on evaluations regularly around the U.S. I know because I have received them as part of packets when I show up to speak. They would be laughable if they didn't cost so much effort with such little valuable information in return.

Why are these the wrong questions to ask? Take a group of people—size of group doesn't matter—and you will have as many different ways of responding to a question of this sort as you have people in a group. There is no rhyme or reason to the answers, people just tell you what they think or feel. You gather a lot of data, but what good is it?

On-the-spot evaluations (aka Don't wait for the questionnaire!)

Remember that the purpose of evaluations is to help you determine the effectiveness of your work, decide what else needs to be done to move the work forward, and to make sure what you are doing achieves the desired outcome. Anything else done with evaluations is secondary or worse. While it is good to know whether your audience was comfortable or uncomfortable, whether they enjoyed the speaker or program or not, or whether babysitting is desired, they are only surface-level questions and should be handled quickly and efficiently and then left to others to address.

On a practical level, questions about the comfort of the meeting room should be handled immediately. Watch your audience. Are they squirming in their seats because their butts are numb from sitting too long? If so, call a break, whether one is scheduled or not. Are men and women pulling on their sweaters or wrapping their arms around their bodies? If so, the room is too cold. Turn down the air conditioning or turn up the heat immediately, if you can. Don't wait for a month to go by to read the evaluation and see what people say. They are telling you with their bodies. If you have doubts, don't be afraid to ask, "Is it too cold (or too hot) in the room?" Trust people to tell you the truth.

The same goes for refreshments or babysitting or whether or not people like the speaker. Watch them closely during the event. Ask them direct questions. You will get the answers you need. If people aren't happy with the refreshments, what can you do about it now? (This applies equally with babysitting.)

Listen and watch carefully. If people are yawning and falling asleep during a presentation or while working on a chapter, you know they are bored. That's all the information you need to know.

A model plan

After all of this, what might a written plan look like? While it could take on many different formats, here's a rough outline for creating an effective confirmation preparation program using ideas presented in this book.

CONFIRMATION BLUEPRINT SUGGESTION

Name clearly what you want to accomplish "Prepare young people to become fully, consciously, and actively engaged in the life and mission of our parish and of the larger Catholic Church."

Determine what needs to be done to accomplish that outcome

Strategic Goals: Get young people

1. committed to the faith
2. actively engaged in the life, liturgy, and ministerial activities of the parish community
3. able to pray on their own and in groups
4. willing to be generous with their time, talent, and treasure
5. growing in their personal relationship with God, through Jesus

And so on—I'm not going to do all the thinking for you, just trying to get you started!

Divide and conquer

Objectives: Each of the items mentioned above becomes your intermediate goal; the things you do to accomplish these goals are your objectives—clearly seen steps in the building process: remember, you accomplish goals by accomplishing objectives. In your plan you need to take each goal separately here and then lay out all of the objectives you need to accomplish if you are to achieve your goal. For each objective you need to determine all of the various things that you need to do to accomplish it as well. For example, you may need to engage the young people in Bible study before you try to get them to pray with the Bible. Will you also need to prepare leaders who are equipped to lead Bible study before you can begin this step? Here's an example of how this might look for a few of these goals:

1. committed to the faith
   - introduce them to stories of saints and modern holy people not yet declared saints
   - introduce them to a life of dedication and service
2. actively engaged in the life, liturgy, and ministerial activities of the parish community
   - give them opportunities to gradually become a part of the adult faith community
   - assign adult mentors and role models—as a subobjective, these mentors and role models need to be identified, verified (background checks) and certified (trained for their roles). This must be accounted for in the plan as well
3. able to pray on their own and in groups

- introduced to Church's prayer treasure chest
- communal prayer opportunities, done well and frequently
- have them practice being prayer leaders for both formal and informal prayer

And so on. What can be done in your setting to achieve these objectives?

Determine which goals need to be done first, and within each goal, how the objectives will build, one upon the other Think also about any preparatory work that might need to be done before you can even begin to accomplish an objective. For example, young people can only engage in the parish's social ministry program if one exists. Such a program might need to be started before you can have young people engage in it.

What will this job cost and how long will it take? Establish budgets and timelines for each objective and each goal. If you know how much it will cost and how long it will take to accomplish each step in your goal, your budget will be realistic.

What training will be needed to do the work? Just as not everyone is a trained carpenter or plumber, not everyone knows how to facilitate a group or lead prayer. How many people will you need to prepare? How will you identify and recruit them? What preparation do they need and how will you prepare them?

Determine the programming you will use for the various tasks Some dioceses require two years of preparation before confirmation. In a systemic approach to confirmation, preparation would begin many years before. The reason for this is that you aren't planning a program to prepare children to receive the sacrament, you are preparing them "to become fully, consciously, and actively engaged in the life and mission of our parish and of the larger Catholic Church," as it says in the mission statement provided at the beginning. So what you are actually developing here is the bones of an active Youth Ministry program in which confirmation is a milestone celebrated along the journey; so while you may choose one program for the active preparation for confirmation, you would probably need multiple tools to achieve the goals and objectives necessary to lay the solid foundation upon which confirmation will be built.

Evaluate, evaluate, evaluate Evaluate at each opportunity. Gather data, analyze it, and use it to judge how well your plan is working. Don't hesitate to make course corrections and minor changes to the plan along the way, based upon this information. Constantly check to make sure you are achieving what you want to accomplish. Every year, assess your satisfaction with the plan and whether major changes are needed.

Stick with it Whatever you do, stick with the plan until you have time to see results. Remember the old British saying: "The proof of the pudding is in the eating." The proof of a successful confirmation plan is, are young people becoming fully, consciously, and actively engaged in the life and mission of our parish and of the larger Catholic Church? Because you know what you set out to accomplish and you have identified success indicators for each of the goals, you have the criteria to measure how well you are doing.

— OF RELATED INTEREST —

Everything about Parish Ministry I Wish I Had Known
KATHY HENDRICKS

This very insightful resource, filled with excellent, wise, and useful tidbits, covers all the practical skills necessary for effective pastoral ministry. It's made richer through Kathy's humorous and hands-on approach.

168 pages | $14.95 | 978-1-58595-199-4

Good News Parish Leadership
Trust-Building Guidelines, Tools, and Ideas
MICHAEL L. PAPESH

Author Michael Papesh highlights four essential elements of good news pastoral leadership: ongoing pastoral planning, discernment decision-making, broad and gracious hospitality, and trust building. A fascinating and challenging book for pastoral leaders, associates, pastoral council members, and all who are involved in and committed to parish life.

280 pages | $19.95 | 978-1-58595-705-7

Dreams and Visions
Pastoral Planning for Lifelong Faith Formation
BILL HUEBSCH

Here, Bill urges parish leaders and ministers to move in the direction of lifelong faith formation by offering parishioners powerful conversion experiences. He also offers a clear and consistent plan for step-by-step growth, with special emphasis on excellent liturgies, strong and effective catechist and teacher formation, and developing households of faith.

160 pages | $14.95 | 978-1-58595-638-8

1-800-321-0411
www.23rdpublications.com

TWENTY THIRD PUBLICATIONS